D. H. LAWRENCE'S LETTERS

TO

BERTRAND RUSSELL

EDITED BY HARRY T. MOORE

GOTHAM BOOK MART

NEW YORK

PRINTED IN THE UNITED STATES OF AMERICA

FOREWORD

THIS BOOK contains the letters D. H. Lawrence wrote to Bertrand Russell during the First World War, and Lawrence's comments on the manuscript outline of a lecture-series Russell had prepared.

This correspondence is not a miscellany: it dramatically tells a story that has a beginning, a middle, and an end. For fullest understanding of this material I have provided background information, I hope not excessively, in the Introduction. Further explanations, for those interested in such matters, are supplied in Appendix B, which gives the reasons for the order in which the letters are arranged and for the conjectural dating of those Lawrence left undated.

I hope that others who read these letters—and they are eminently re-readable—will find them as rewarding as I have found them. I also hope that their publication will help toward the long overdue revival of interest in Lawrence. Readers do not have to agree with Lawrence's ideas to find him one of the richest,

v

most exalting reading experiences in the modern world—it is difficult to believe that so many people who like literature have been depriving themselves of Lawrence's poems and novels.

Meanwhile, here is another contribution to Lawrence literature, one of the last important collections of Lawrenciana. This book is the idea of Miss Frances Steloff of the Gotham Book Mart, who owns these letters. I am grateful to her for assigning me this pleasantest of editorial tasks. She and I are in turn grateful to Mrs. Frieda Lawrence and to Mr. Bertrand Russell for making publication of these letters possible. And my wife Beatrice Reynolds Moore deserves my special thanks for her encouragement and practical assistance.

HARRY T. MOORE

Babson Institute
Wellesley Hills, Mass.

CONTENTS

D. H. LAWRENCE'S LETTERS

TO

BERTRAND RUSSELL

INTRODUCTION

THE ANTAGONISTIC FRIENDSHIP of D. H. Lawrence and Bertrand Russell endured for a little more than a year.

Not long after they met in 1915, the two men planned to give a series of lectures together in London. Both Lawrence and Russell were opposed to war and were distressed by the one then going on in Europe. But instead of establishing a common front, they became involved in a little war of their own. Its story is told in these twenty-three letters from Lawrence to Russell.

They contain some of Lawrence's most intense utterances, for during that period (early 1915 to early 1916) he was going through a tormenting spiritual crisis.

It was not only the war that agitated him: 1915 was the year in which the most important book he had yet written was suppressed because a magistrate decreed that this novel was indecent. For several years after the trouble over *The Rainbow*, Lawrence found it almost impossible to earn money by writing, and he had no other income. Later in the war he was to become so poor that he could not afford to buy fuel for his cottage—he had to burn chips he picked up after trees had been cut down for use in the war industries. Another cause of wretchedness at the time was the hatred that he felt was being directed against him by the authorities and by people in general because his wife was German.

Most of Lawrence's closest friends during those troubled years were aristocrats. With the exception of John Middleton Murry and Katherine Mansfield, young writers who had not yet come so far as he had along the road to recognition, Lawrence's chief correspondents and associates during the period were Lady Ottoline Morrell and Lady Cynthia Asquith. Lawrence had a faculty similar to that of his German contemporary, Rilke, for arousing sympathy in high-born women. Lawrence's wife, *geb.* Frieda von Richthofen, was a baroness.

Like Lawrence's influential women friends Lady Ottoline and Lady Cynthia, Bertrand Russell belonged to one of the great families of England, yet Lawrence, the coal miner's son, had achieved enough to make him feel entitled to regard Russell and himself as fellow-workers in the vineyard. The egalitarian who had written *Sons and Lovers* and a number of highly praised poems and stories felt he could assume with Russell the you-and-I-are-intellectuals-together attitude.

Not that Lawrence in his proudest moments could have seriously compared his own accomplishments up to that time with those of Russell. A few years before, Russell had collaborated

with Alfred North Whitehead on *Principia Mathematica*, recognized from the first as one of the masterpieces in its field.
Russell had written other important books, and his position on
the faculty at Cambridge University no doubt impressed Lawrence, who had not yet developed his contempt for professors
and erudition. In his youth Lawrence had been an excellent
student, had earned a high-school scholarship, and had one year
stood first in all England and Wales in the Uncertified Teachers'
Examination. His own record as a schoolmaster was a good one:
this man who was to become one of the age's most ferocious
enemies of science had been a successful teacher of science.

Lawrence had given up teaching in 1912 because of poor
health. From then on he made his living only by writing, though
from time to time he accepted donations from friends. Letter
Number 22 of the present volume, which asks Russell to remember him in his will, provides an example of the outrageous
coyness with which Lawrence could occasionally ask for money.

At the time of the first letters to Russell, who had been introduced to the Lawrences by Lady Ottoline, the Lawrences were
living in a cottage at Greatham, in Sussex. They had been stay-
ing in Bucks, where during an illness Lawrence had grown the
red beard he wore the rest of his life; it gave him the look of a
prophet and it later symbolized his 'isolate manhood.'

Lawrence wrote to a friend in Nottingham about the new
home in Sussex:

It is the Meynell's place. You know Alice Meynell, Catholic poetess,

[3]

rescuer of Francis Thompson. The father took a big old farm house at Greatham, then proceeded to give each of his children a cottage. Now Viola lends us hers.*

The first letter of the present series (and a highly important letter for the understanding of Lawrence) is dated '12 Feb. 1915' and is addressed to 'Dear Mr. Russell.' Lawrence's salutations in this correspondence tell an interesting part of the story. They go from this Dear Mr. Russell to Dear Bertrand Russell and Dear Russell, then, after a break, to a heartier Dear Bertie, and at last to the formal extreme of My Dear Russell. Lawrence, despite all his cheekiness, always felt smirched by the coal-grit of the Nottingham mines, and even in his freest moments with Russell he could not quite shake off the collier's-boy-before-the-son-of-the-manor-house attitude.

At the beginning of the friendship Lawrence told Lady Ottoline Morrel (apparently in early March, 1915), 'Bertrand Russell wrote me. I feel a quickening of love for him.' Huxley on page 235 of his edition places this letter, datelined only 'Monday,' after May 31, which is wrong by nearly three months. Lawrence in the text of the letter mentions the visit he will make to Cambridge at the end of that week; it appears that he made only one visit there, during the first weekend of March of 1915. Appendix B of the present volume, where reasons are given for the affixing of dates to various letters on the basis of internal

* The Letters of D. H. Lawrence, edited by Aldous Huxley (New York: The Viking Press, 1932), p. 219. Hereafter this collection will be itemized as Huxley.

[4]

evidence, discusses Lawrence's disillusionment with Cambridge, which comes out in Letter Number 5 of the Russell correspondence. Lawrence also speaks slightingly of Cambridge several times in letters in the Huxley volume (pages 238 and 390). And Frieda Lawrence, in her memoir of her husband, states that 'he had expected much' of his Cambridge visit, but that when he returned he said: 'Well, in the evening they drank port and they walked up and down the room and talked about the Balkan situation and things like that, and they know nothing about it.'*

Russell returned Lawrence's visit toward the end of June. Lawrence's letter to Lady Ottoline on page 242 of the Huxley edition, dated only 'Sunday,' tells her that Russell is at Greatham. Since the weekend of June 19 is mentioned twice in the Lawrence-Russell correspondence in the present volume, the letter in Huxley may safely be dated Sunday, June 20, 1915. Lawrence complains to Lady Ottoline that Russell, 'apart from philosophical mathematics,' tends to be limited by the immediate and the temporal and does not enter into the knowledge of the Absolute. Lawrence, however, believes that he is giving Russell a sense of eternity. He tells Lady Ottoline of their plan for the London lectures; Russell will speak on ethics, Lawrence on immortality, and they will establish a kind of religious society, centered in the knowledge of God. This will lead to 'action.'

Lawrence wants Lady Ottoline to be president of the society,

*Frieda Lawrence, 'Not I, But The Wind . . .' (Santa Fé: The Rydal Press, 1934), p. 100.

and he wants also to draw in Gilbert Cannan (who was in a few years to be certified as insane), Gordon Campbell (afterward Lord Glenavy), and the 'Murrys' (Murry and Katherine Mansfield, later to be married). Lawrence suggests meetings at Garsington, Lady Ottoline's estate in Oxfordshire, which is 'like that Boccaccio place where they told all the Decamerone.'

Apparently that weekend of June 19-20 was the time when the Lawrence-Russell lecture series was first thought of. It now seems strange that these two men, so antipodal in temperament, decided to give joint lectures. At the time they had a feeling of fellowship, however: it has already been mentioned that both of them were opposed to war, and that both had been shaken up by the coming of the First World War. Russell wrote in 1927:

I had watched with growing anxiety the policies of all the European great powers in the years before 1914, and was quite unable to accept the superficial melodramatic explanations of the catastrophe which were promulgated by the belligerent governments. . . . Civilization, which I had thought secure, showed itself capable of generating destructive forces which threatened a disaster comparable to the fall of Rome.*

And in 1930 he stated:

I have never been so whole-hearted or so little troubled with hesitation in any work as in the pacifist work that I did during the war. For the first time I found something to do which involved my whole nature. My previous abstract work had left my human interests unsatisfied, and I had allowed them an occasional outlet by political speaking and

* *Selected Papers of Bertrand Russell* (New York: The Modern Library, 1927), pp. xi-xii.

writing, more particularly on free trade and votes for women. The aristocratic political tradition of the eighteenth and early nineteenth centuries, which I had imbibed in childhood, had made me feel an instinctive responsibility in regard to public affairs. And a strong parental instinct, at that time not satisfied in a personal way, caused me to feel a great indignation at the spectacle of the young men of Europe being deceived and butchered in order to gratify the evil passions of their elders.*

Lawrence had been walking in Westmorland, 'rather happy, with water-lilies twisted round [his] hat,' when he received news of the outbreak of war. He described what he had felt at that time, in a letter to Lady Cynthia Asquith the following January 30; he told her that the war 'was a spear through the side of all sorrows and hopes.' Things had ceased to exist for him; he felt that his soul was in the tomb, with a stone over it, and that neither he nor anyone else existed. But he knew he would rise again.

This description of his spiritual death is of course partly hyperbole, though other letters preceding this one, and the testimony of Lawrence's friends, bear out that he was miserable at the time. The letter to Lady Cynthia was written shortly after the Lawrences arrived at Greatham; the coming resurrection he speaks of had its first stirrings as he walked on the Sussex downs. By the 1st of February he was writing to Lady Ottoline in a vein prophetic of the one he was to write her in (as we have already seen) six months later; he tells her in this February 1 letter that

*Bertrand Russell and others, *What I Believe* (New York: Simon and Schuster, 1931), pp. 12-13.

[7]

she must be the center of a new community which will inspire a new kind of life 'in which the only riches is integrity of character.' This leads directly to the Russell correspondence, which begins later that month: and, as we have seen, the men are by June planning the lecture series.

By July 9, Lawrence is telling Lady Ottoline that Russell, who has mailed him the synopsis of his lectures on Political Ideals, still needs to break away from the shore of 'this existing world' in a boat 'and preach from out the waters of eternity.' He hopes that Russell is not angry with him. And although he has stopped writing his own philosophy until he is 'freer,' he feels hopeful for *The Rainbow* as he corrects proof on it. He continues the seafaring metaphor: this novel 'is the voyage of discovery towards the real and eternal and unknown land.'

And he spoke truly there: *The Rainbow* was a new beginning for him. After *Sons and Lovers* the way was open for Lawrence to become one of the most popular of English novelists, perhaps a successor to Meredith with the wide public that likes well-written novels which are not too disturbing. Lawrence had a supreme gift for evoking his native landscape, and he had a Dickens-like talent for bringing a character to life with a few deft strokes: if he merely exploited his skill along these lines, he would have fame, comfort, and wealth.

But this was not Lawrence's way: he felt the challenge to go in another direction, to explore the phases of human consciousness that previous novels had not explored. All this was in the

Zeitgeist, for it was only a few years since Freud had pried open the Pandora's box of the Unconscious. Other novelists had been working in consciousness-experiment techniques, those writers who were Henry James's spiritual descendants—Joyce, Proust, and Dorothy Richardson. But Lawrence's experiments were of a different kind, since these authors were for the most part investigating the mental aspects of consciousness. Lawrence was exploring almost entirely its *emotional* properties. And the lyricism which had from the first characterized his work was now becoming infused with mysticism.

Russell was three years later to publish his attack on mysticism, the book called *Mysticism and Logic*. Once when a young writer (William Gerhardi) asked Russell if he ever resorted to mysticism, Russell replied 'Yes, when I am humiliated.'

He and Lawrence differed on so many points that it would be interesting to have a record of their conversations, at Garsington, London, Cambridge, and Greatham—what they said in the give-and-take element of talk must have been quite as interesting as what they wrote in letters. It is regrettable that Russell's letters were not preserved, but his responses can be conjectured, partly from Lawrence's own letters and partly from Russell's known philosophic stand. Appendix A shows how completely the two men agreed or dissented on various important issues.

Their main quarrel can be most simply described as one between emotion and mind—or, in somewhat more philosophic nomenclature, it can be called a quarrel between instinct (or intuition) and reason (or intellect). Lawrence in 1913, not long after completing *Sons and Lovers*, stated in a letter what was essentially to be his philosophy for the rest of his life: 'My great religion is a belief in the blood, the flesh, as being wiser than the intellect. We can go wrong in our minds. But what our blood feels and believes and says, is always true.' (Huxley, p. 96.)

In 1914 Russell had written, in *Our Knowledge of the External World* (delivered as lectures at American universities):

The theoretical understanding of the world, which is the aim of philosophy, is not a matter of great practical importance to animals, or to savages, or even to most civilized men. It is hardly to be supposed, therefore, that the rapid, rough and ready methods of instinct or intuition will find in this field a favorable ground for their application. It is the older kinds of activity, which bring out our kinship with remote generations of animal and semi-human ancestors, that show intuition at its best. In such matters as self-preservation and love, intuition will act sometimes (though not always) with a swiftness and precision which are astonishing to the critical intellect. But philosophy is not one of the pursuits which illustrate our affinity with the past: it is a highly refined, highly civilized pursuit, demanding, for its success, a certain liberation from the life of instinct, and even, at times, a certain aloofness from all mundane hopes and fears. It is not in philosophy, therefore, that we can hope to see intuition at its best. On the contrary, since the true objects of philosophy, and the habits of thought demanded for their apprehension, are strange, unusual, and remote, it is here, more almost than anywhere else, that intellect proves superior to intuition, and that quick unanalyzed convictions are least deserving of uncritical acceptance.*

* *Selected Papers of Bertrand Russell*, pp. 340-341.

[10]

The recurrence of such passages in Russell's writing shows how far removed he was from Lawrence's 'blood-consciousness' philosophy. Perhaps it was that parental instinct which Russell ascribes to himself which made him remain friendly to Lawrence for as long as he did, and certainly Lawrence felt a tenderness for Russell, as the quotations from Lawrence's letters in the foregoing have shown.

Along with that tenderness, Lawrence also felt exasperation at times. In another letter to Lady Ottoline Morrell (Huxley places this before June 1 but, as I show in Appendix B of the present volume, we now have evidence that it should be given a July date), Lawrence says that Russell is really too callow, that he writes 'lachrymose letters' full of a disillusionment that seems juvenile, and that he should 'clench his fist in the face of the world.'

Lawrence was at this time twenty-nine years old; Russell was forty-three.

At the beginning of August 1915 the Lawrences left Greatham and took a flat in the Hampstead section of London. Earlier in the month they went up to the city to look for furniture. Lawrence talked with Russell and wrote Lady Ottoline a letter headed 'Monday,' probably July 12, which tells of his disagreement with Russell about 'the Infinite, the Absolute,' which Lawrence felt to be the 'starting point . . . on the journey toward Truth.' But, Lawrence reports, the two of them 'have almost sworn *Blutbrüderschaft.*'

On the 26th of July—Letter Number 12 of the present set—Lawrence is scolding Russell. Ten days later he sends a short, friendlier note (Number 13), though he is 'dislocated and unhappy' after the move. On August 16, Lawrence tells Lady Cynthia Asquith that he does not know whether the lectures will ever begin: 'I don't see how I am to start. Russell and I were to do something together. He was to give a *real* course on political reconstruction ideas. But it is no good. He sent me a synopsis of the lectures, and I can only think them pernicious. And now his vanity is piqued, because I said they *must* be different. . . . What does Russell really want? He wants to keep his own established ego, his finite and ready-defined self intact, free from contact and connection. He wants to be ultimately a free agent. That is what they all want ultimately—that is what is at the back of all peace-for-ever and democratic control talk . . .' (Huxley, pp. 250-251)—and he rails on for several more pages. Once he says he feels like 'running off to some unformed South American place'—one of the first stirrings, perhaps, of the idea he was to develop later that year, of establishing an 'ideal' colony in the Western Hemisphere. In complaining to Lady Cynthia that Russell's vanity was piqued because Lawrence said the lectures *must* be different, Lawrence failed to mention that when he had used that imperative (in the third paragraph of Letter Number 11, 'You *must* work out the idea of a new state . . .'), he had underlined the brusque little word fifteen times.

Then, on the same day that he writes Letter Number 14 to

Russell—September 5—Lawrence tells Lady Cynthia that he has quarreled deeply with Russell and that there will probably be no lectures. Russell finally gave his own series.

Lawrence is now starting the magazine *The Signature*, in association with Murry and Katherine Mansfield, as he tells both Russell and Lady Cynthia on that day (September 5), inviting Russell to be a contributor.

Four days later Lawrence informs Lady Ottoline that he and Russell have parted; it is 'for a little while,' and 'only in the natural course. The real development continues even in its negation, under the winter.' But on the 14th of September he writes Russell a blistering, accusatory letter, Number 15 in the present volume, telling Lady Ottoline about it on the same day (p. 258 in Huxley's collection). It has made Lawrence both glad and sorry, he informs her, to have written this letter, but it also has made him want to find a corner to cry in, as when he was a child. But by the 20th of September, when he tells Lady Cynthia about it, he is feeling better, and the air is clearer, as after a thunderstorm. Lawrence wrote across Russell's synopsis of the lectures his own disagreement with Russell's ideas; Russell's synopsis of his own set of lectures and Lawrence's comments are printed in Appendix A of the present volume.

Lawrence's 'little paper,' *The Signature*, was part of his relationship with Murry, which was a counterpoise to his relationship with Russell.

[13]

Ten years afterward, Lawrence spoke somewhat jeeringly of *The Signature*, which he credits Murry with suggesting:

To me the venture meant nothing real: a little escapade. I don't believe in 'doing things' like that. In a great issue like the war, there was nothing to be 'done,' in Murry's sense. There is still nothing to be 'done.' Probably not for many, many years will men start to 'do' something. And even then, only after they have changed gradually, and deeply.*

Murry complained, in a book written after Lawrence's death, that this statement was unfair. But Lawrence's correspondence at the time does not indicate that he felt very much enthusiasm for the project; it is true that he tried to induce friends to find subscribers among 'those who cared' for 'the living truth,' and once he expressed the hope that *The Signature* would be the seed of a great new life, but in the main there is little earnestness in his appeals—he seems less worked up about the magazine than he had been about the lectures.

Yet Lawrence's essay which appeared in *The Signature's* three numbers—'The Crown'—represented his serious thinking at the time; and ten years later he still cleaved to it essentially. But he also stated that it was 'ridiculous' to offer this essay 'in a little sixpenny pamphlet. I always felt ashamed, at the thought of the few who sent their half-crowns. Happily they were few, and they could read Murry.'†

*D. H. Lawrence, *Reflections on the Death of a Porcupine and Other Essays* (Philadelphia: The Centaur Press, 1925). Pages in the introductory 'Note' are unnumbered.

†*Ibid.*, 'Note.'

Lawrence said that 'The Crown' is 'no use for a five minutes' lunch'—and the present Introduction is in any event not the appropriate place for a précis of that essay or a discussion of its somewhat Manichean symbolism. The reader who studies it in the *Porcupine* volume will find a relationship between it and the Russell letters, though Lawrence revised the essay before it appeared in that book so long afterward.

Murry's contribution to the three issues of *The Signature* was an essay called 'There Was a Little Man.' In it he expressed his attitude to the war: 'Passionately and from the depths of my heart I say "This monstrous thing does not exist"; there is no real relation between it and me.'

It is interesting to consider the attitude to war that was held over the years by these three men, Lawrence, Murry, and Russell.

Lawrence, in the chapter of *Kangaroo* called 'The Nightmare,' has told of his experiences on the occasions when he was called up to be examined for military service. This is one of the most vital descriptions of the backstage side of modern warfare that has yet been written: Lawrence was known to be an objector to war, and he was married to a German. A thin little man when he took off his clothes and stood among the healthier specimens, he felt that the doctors were trying to 'do him down'—and possibly they were. In *Kangaroo*, Lawrence's autobiographical character Somers goes up to his native Midlands for one of his examinations:

[15]

He wondered what instructions they had had about him. Oh, foul dogs. But they were very close on him now, very close. They were grinning very close behind him, like hyaenas just going to bite. Yes, they were running him to earth. They had exposed all his nakedness to jibes. And they were pining, almost whimpering to give the last grab at him, and haul him to earth, a victim. Finished!

But not yet! Oh, no, not yet. Not yet, not now, nor ever. Not while life was life, should they lay hold of him. Never again. Never would he be touched again. And because they had handled his private parts, and looked into them, their eyes should burst and their hands should wither and their hearts should rot. So he cursed them in his blood, with an unremitting curse. . . . He would obey no more, not one more stride. If they summoned him he would disappear: or find some means of fighting them. But no more obedience: no more presenting himself when called up. By God, no! Never while he lived again, would he be at the disposal of society.*

This emotion recollected in untranquility was recorded some years later at the remove of Australia: *Kangaroo*, one of Lawrence's least known and most profound novels, is a forcible statement of individualism—and it is a book which indicates that, although *some* parts of his doctrine *at times* apparently resembled *some* parts of the Nazi doctrine, Lawrence would have never advocated the realization of Nazism. In a police state Lawrence would have hated the brutality more than most people do, and he would have hated the muzzling more than anyone.

*D. H. Lawrence, *Kangaroo* (New York: Thomas Selzer, 1923), pp. 300-301.

Whether Lawrence would have supported the Allied cause in the Second World War is a matter inviting conjecture. He was certainly no more deeply pacifist than Russell, who did support that cause. But it is debatable whether Lawrence would have favored the large-scale bombing of cities or the use of the atom bomb: we must remember how his spokesman-character in *Aaron's Rod*, Rawdon Lilly, puts Aaron out of his flat because Aaron has defended the use of poison gas.

Yet these speculations as to what Lawrence's attitude might be today are speculations in a void. It must be remembered that from the time of Lawrence's death to the moment when England and Germany were at war again, Europe passed through a tormented decade.

It was a decade that changed many men besides Russell, whose 1916 collection of esssays, *Justice in War Time*, challenged the British war aims and criticized the nation's foreign policy. Russell was dismissed from his post at Trinity College, Cambridge, his library was seized, and he was denied a passport to America. He was imprisoned for four and a half months in 1918 (and while serving his sentence wrote *Introduction to Mathematical Philosophy*), for condemning the use of American troops to quell labor disputes—under the Defense of the Realm act, the article he published on the subject was considered endangering to Anglo-American unity, although the material that the article was based on came from an official publication of the United States Government.

Russell's attitude toward the Allied aims in the Second World War was, as I have already mentioned, quite different: he supported the opponents of Nazism. And he became once again a member of the faculty at Cambridge. He had inherited his earldom, though he does not himself use the title. His recent beliefs about war and the future of mankind have been partly expressed in an article in a British magazine; in this he has stated his belief in the possibility that humanity, although on the edge of self-destruction, can yet be persuaded to take measures for survival. In Russell's allowance, these measures will have to be militant:

It is entirely clear that there is only one way in which great wars can be permanently prevented, and that is the establishment of an international government with a monopoly of serious armed force. When I speak of an international government, I mean one that really governs, not an amiable façade like the League of Nations, or a pretentious sham like the United Nations under its present constitution. An international government, if it is to be able to preserve peace, must have the only atomic bombs, the only plant for producing them, the only air force, the only battleships, and, generally, whatever is necessary to make it irresistible. Its atomic staff, its air squadrons, the crews of its battleships, and its infantry regiments must each severally be composed of men of many different nations; there must be no possibility of a development of national feeling in any unit larger than a company. Every member of the international armed force should be carefully trained in loyalty to the international government.*

Now, to complete the picture, what of Lawrence's other close

*'The Atomic Bomb and the Prevention of War,' Polemic, No. 4 (July-August 1946), pp. 16-17.

[18]

friend of the 1915-16 period, Murry? His mutations are hard to follow because on every question he has changed so often, and in so many different directions. His intellectual chameleonism has kept him from centralizing his talents on the activity for which he is best fitted—literary criticism. His temperament has led him down by-paths of nebulous theology and anagogic socialism. In spite of this he has accomplished much; his studies of Keats and his *The Problem of Style* should assure him of a place among the better English critics of this half-century—these books will certainly outlive his reputation for confused evangelism.

Nothing so decisively indicates Murry's continual switching about as his attitudes to war. For, *after* taking a stand with Lawrence against the continuance of the First World War ('This monstrous thing does not exist'), he went into the Admiralty on a kind of public-relations assignment and emerged with an Order of Merit. But in the Second World War, Murry was a Dick Sheppard pacifist.

Lawrence seems from the first to have had an inkling of Murry's tendency to be anfractuous; partly, his affection for Murry kept him from realizing the worst possibilities of the tendency. Lawrence's assurance to Lady Ottoline in the summer of 1915 does not quite have the ring of a firm assurance: 'Murry has a genuine side to his nature: so has Mrs. Murry. Don't mistrust them. They are valuable, I know.' (Huxley, p. 243.)

[19]

The crisis of antagonism between Lawrence and Murry was not to be reached until the following spring, in Cornwall. But during the previous summer and autumn, Lawrence seemed gradually to lose interest in the magazine venture with Murry, as his correspondence at the time shows.

Lawrence had other matters to fill his mind. One was the publication of *The Rainbow* and its suppression; the other was the scheme for going to America.

The Rainbow came out at the end of September and was suppressed early in November. Some of Lawrence's friends rallied to him; others disappointed him. Catherine Carswell lost her reviewing assignment on the Glasgow *Herald* for having praised the book. Philip Morrell, Lady Ottoline's husband, asked a question in Parliament about the suppression. Lawrence wrote Cynthia Asquith to inquire whether she and her husband (son of the Prime Minister) could help; Lawrence reproachfully informed Lady Cynthia that the book was not indecent, although he had heard of her commenting in shocked tones that it was 'much worse' than the second story in Lawrence's earlier volume, *The Prussian Officer*. And Lawrence wrote Edward Marsh on November 6, telling him that although he jeered at *The Rainbow*, it was one of the great English novels ('I tell you, who know'). Lawrence said he was sick, dreading another winter, and wanted to go to Florida. Although he owed Marsh ten pounds he needed more, would pay it back if he ever made any money;

he would give Marsh, who edited the *Georgian Verse* annual, permanent possession of some of his future poems.

Money troubles (Marsh generously sent twenty pounds) were not all that lay ahead of Lawrence: after the trip to Utopia was planned, he and his wife were not allowed to leave England. When he finally did get out, in 1919, Lawrence never went back again except for brief unhappy visits.

After a lapse of two months, the correspondence with Russell resumes on November 17, 1915, with Letter Number 16, evidently written in response to an invitation to dinner. At the end of November, Lawrence and Russell are at Garsington together with some other guests. In December, Lawrence writes Lady Ottoline that he again has hopes for 'Bertie,' who is 'growing *much better*' and is 'going to become young and new.' In Letter 18 to Russell, December 8, Lawrence is back at his blood-consciousness philosophy again, and is giving Russell a comprehensive sermon on the subject. However antagonizing this may have been to Russell, it is one of the great Lawrence letters, and an important statement of doctrine he was developing. The next letter, in this volume conjecturally dated December 23, invites Russell to join the half-dozen or so young people in the Florida venture.

The January 13 letter, Number 20, is one of the friendliest of all, with its 'Dear Bertie' salutation and its cordial first paragraph. Lawrence is now in Cornwall, a place with a stimulating effect upon his writing power, and he gives Russell some word-pictures of the landscape, its inhabitants, and its atmosphere. This kind of impressionism is unusual in Lawrence's letters to Russell, for in most of them Lawrence mutes his customary descriptive utterances and keeps to philosophical discussion, although this is often presented in the same urgent, repetitive rhythms as his descriptions.

The two men mentioned in Letter 20 as being with the Lawrences were among the young people in the Florida venture, though they were soon to get out of the Lawrence camp. Philip Heseltine was the composer who was later to use the pseudonym Peter Warlock; Dikrān Kouzoumdjian, already the author of two books written under his Armenian patrilineal name, was afterward to become famous as Michael Arlen.

Lawrence writes to Russell again, a month afterward, and this time he tells about the book-publishing scheme, of which Heseltine has been the leading inciter. Then, a little later, Lawrence has received a communication from Russell which he speaks of in a February 15 letter to Lady Ottoline: Russell had sounded miserable, wondering why he went on living, and though his lectures had been financially successful, they had had no important influence. Only pride and obstinacy, Russell had told Lawrence, kept him alive.

Lawrence a few days later (Letter 22) writes Russell slashingly, but with 'love to you.' The following month he tries again, in a cordial letter with a formal salutation and a friendly sugges-

[22]

tion of another visit to the Lawrences—and Russell seems never to have answered.

What is the sequel?

It is largely the kind of small sniping that can be amusing and that is often interesting.

Lawrence makes a few references to his former friend in his later correspondence. He speaks sneeringly to Lady Cynthia in December 1916 of 'that old advanced crowd—Cambridge, Lowes Dickenson [sic], Bertie Russell, young reformers, Socialists, Fabians—they are our disease, not our hope.' (Huxley, p. 390.)

The friendship with Lady Ottoline faded, too, and when Lawrence in bitterness wrote *Women in Love* during 1916, in stony Cornwall, he made her a monstrous character in the story. (This was the final version of his old novel, *The Sisters*, begun in the Tyrol three years before; *The Rainbow* was also an off-shoot of *The Sisters*). And although *Women in Love* was completed in the middle of the war, it was not published in England until 1921—and then there was consternation, when Lady Ottoline recognized herself as Hermione Roddice, Heseltine discovered himself as the decadent bohemian Halliday, and other former friends of Lawrence found themselves diligently lampooned.

In the story, Hermione presides over a Midlands estate, Bredalby, which is really Garsington. She is herself portrayed as one of the female types Lawrence abhorred most—the will-driven woman. In one particularly intense scene she tries to brain the Lawrence-man, Rupert Birkin, with a lump of lapis-lazuli, but he holds a volume of Thucydides before his skull and fends off the blow. Lawrence, in one of his 1916 letters to Lady Ottoline, thanks her for sending him a volume of Thucydides.

Russell also appears to be caricatured in *Women in Love*, recognizable among the guests at Bredalby as Sir Joshua Malleson, 'a learned, dry Baronet of fifty, who was always making witticisms and laughing at them heartily in a harsh, horse-laugh. . . . [His] mental fibre was so tough as to be insentient.' The stiff-bodied 'elderly sociologist' comes in for some more jibes and in some of the discussions his statements are parodies of points in the Russell philosophy—and he is of course confuted by the brilliant Rupert Birkin.

Lawrence and Lady Ottoline were reconciled in 1928, when he was composing *Lady Chatterley's Lover* in Italy. He wrote her the kind of letter he sometimes bestowed on people whom he had cruelly put into his books—people for whom he often felt a nostalgic affection long afterward. He assured her that she was a magnificent woman, an influence of great importance in many lives. She was generous, she stirred the imagination, and he wished they were all back at Garsington, starting afresh.

In one of his subsequent letters to her there is a final mention of Russell: 'I was glad to hear of Bertie Russell. Perhaps he and his Dora will do something, after all—better than his donning away in Cambridge.' (Huxley, p. 792.)

Since Lawrence's death, Russell has a few times referred to him in his writings; he has sometimes attacked Lawrence philosophically. In *A History of Western Philosophy* (1945), Russell mentions Lawrence, without particularly condemning him, as a progeny of the romantic movement.

One malicious echo of the Lawrence-Russell relationship comes at second hand (or second ear) from an anecdote. William Gerhardi, who had written a clever little novel called *The Polyglots*, was introduced around British literary circles in the middle 1920's as a bright young man, and he met both Lawrence and Russell. He tells in his autobiography of talking with Russell during a weekend at H. G. Wells's Easton Glebe:

...Bertrand Russell, whose eyes gleamed with loving-kindness, answered my discreet inquiries into the realm of the Mind with the utmost willingness and lucidity. Only when I mentioned D. H. Lawrence's theories did the look of serenity fade in his large wise eyes, and a note of intellectual fastidiousness crept into his voice, and he said 'Lawrence has no mind.' He referred to the letters Lawrence wrote to him during the war, and how, of course, he, Bertrand Russell, was not going to be instructed in wisdom by D. H. Lawrence. A week later, meeting Lawrence, I told him how enchanted I had been by the lucidity, the suppleness and pliability of Bertrand Russell's mind. He sniffed. 'Have you ever seen him in a bathing-dress?' he asked. 'Poor Bertie Russell! He is all Disembodied Mind!'*

These two statements, 'Lawrence has no mind' and 'Poor

*William Gerhardi, *Memoirs of a Polyglot* (New York: Alfred A. Knopf, 1931), p. 234.

Bertie Russell is all Disembodied Mind,' epitomize the differences between the two men and provide the most effective epitaph to the disenchanted relationship of the mystagogic poet and the mathematic logician.

D. H. LAWRENCE'S LETTERS
TO BERTRAND RUSSELL

Words that Lawrence crossed out are enclosed in French quotation marks » «. Bracketed dates in the letters' headings are the editor's conjectures, which are explained in Appendix B.

GREATHAM,

PULBOROUGH,

SUSSEX.

12 Feb 1915

DEAR MR. RUSSELL,

We have had E. M. Forster here for three days. There is more in him than ever comes out. But he is not dead yet. I hope to see him pregnant with his own soul. We were on the edge of a fierce quarrel all the time. He went to bed muttering that he was not sure we—my wife & I—were n't just playing round his knees: he seized a candle & went to bed, neither would he say good night. Which I think is rather nice. He sucks his dummy—you know, those child's comforters—long after his age. But there is something very real in him, if he will not cause it to die. He is *much* more than his dummy-sucking, clever little habits allow him to be.

I write to say to you that we *must* start a solid basis of freedom of actual living—not only of thinking. We *must* provide another standard than the pecuniary standard, to measure *all* daily life by. We must be free of the economic question. Economic life must be the means to actual life. We must make it so at once.

There must be a revolution in the state. It shall begin by the nationalising of all »radio« industries and means of communication, & of the land—in one fell blow. Then a man shall have his wages whether he is sick or well or old—if anything prevents his working, he shall have his wages just the same. So we shall not live in fear of the wolf—no man amongst us, & no woman, shall have any fear of the wolf at the door, for all wolves are dead.

Which practically solves the whole economic question for the present. All dispossessed owners shall receive a proportionate income—no capital recompense—for the space of, say fifty years.

Something like this must be done. It is no use saying a man's soul should be free, if his boots hurt him so much he can't walk. All our ideals are cant & hypocrisy till we have burst the fetters of this money. Titan nailed on the rock of the modern industrial capitalistic system, declaring in fine language that his soul is free as the Oceanids that fly away on »the« wings of aspiration, while the bird of carrion desire gluts at his liver, is too shameful. I am ashamed to write any real writing of passionate love to my fellow men. Only satire is decent now. The rest is a lie. Until we act, move, rip ourselves off the rock. So there must be an actual revolution, to set free our bodies. For there never was a free soul in a chained body. That is a lie. There might be a resigned soul. But a resigned soul is not a free soul. A resigned soul has yielded its claim on temporal living. It can only do this because the temporal living is being done for it vicariously. Therefore it is dependent on the vicar, let it say what it will. So Christ, who resigned his life, only resigned it because he knew the others would keep theirs. They would do the living, & would later adapt his method to their living. The freedom of the soul within the »chained« denied body is a sheer conceit.

Forster is not poor, but he is bound hand & foot bodily. Why? *Because he does not believe that any beauty or any divine utterance is any good any more.* Why? Because the world is suffering from bonds, and birds of foul desire which gnaw its liver. Forster knows, as every thinking man now knows, that all his thinking and his passion for humanity amounts to no more than trying to soothe with poetry a man raging with pain which can be cured. Cure the pain, don't give the poetry. Will all the poetry in the world satisfy the manhood of Forster, when Forster knows that his implicit manhood is to be satisfied by nothing but immediate physical action. He tries to dodge himself—the sight is pitiful.

But why can't he act? Why can't he take a woman and fight clear to his own basic, primal being? Because he knows that self-realisation is not his ultimate desire. His ultimate desire is for the continued action which has been called the social passion— the love for humanity—the desire to work for humanity. That is every man's ultimate desire & need. Now you see the vicious circle. Shall I go to my Prometheus and tell him beautiful tales of the free, whilst the vulture gnaws his liver? I am ashamed. I turn my face aside from my Prometheus, ashamed of my vain, irrelevant, impudent words. I cannot help Prometheus. And this knowledge rots the love of activity.

If I cannot help Prometheus—and I am also Prometheus— how shall I be able to take a woman? For I go to a woman to know myself, and to know her. And I want to know myself, that

I may know how to act for humanity. But if I am aware that I cannot act for humanity—? Then I dare not go to a woman.

Because, if I go, I know I shall betray myself & her & everything. It will be a vicious circle. I go to her to know myself, & I know myself—what?—to enjoy myself. That is sensationalism—that I go to a woman to »know« feel myself only. Love is, that I go to a woman to know myself, & knowing myself, to go further, to explore in to the unknown, which is the woman, venture in upon the coasts of the unknown, and open my discovery to all humanity. But if I know that humanity is lame & cannot move, bound and in pain and unable to come along, my offering it discoveries is only a cynicism. Which I know & Forster knows & even Gilbert Cannan knows. "They can't hear you," Gilbert Cannan says of the public. "They turn you into a sensation." So he panders to the chained Prometheus, tickles him with near sensations—a beastly thing to do. He writes Young Earnest.

If I know that humanity is chained to a rock, I cannot set set [sic] forth to find it new lands to enter upon. If I do pretend to set forth, I am a cheating, false merchant, seeking my *own* ends. And I am ashamed to be that. I will not.

So then, how shall I come to a woman? To know myself first. Well and good. But knowing myself is only preparing myself. What for? For the adventure into the unexplored, the woman, the whatever-it-is I am up against.—Then the actual heart says "No no — I can't explore. Because an explorer is one sent forth from a great body of people to open out new lands for their occupation. But my people cannot even move—it is chained—paralysed. I am not an explorer. I am a curious, inquisitive man with eyes that can only look for something to take back with him. And what can I take back with me? Not revelation—only curios—titillations. I am a curio hunter. ["]

Again, I am ashamed.

Well then, I am neither explorer nor curio hunter. What then? For what do I come to a woman? To know myself. But what when I know myself? What do I then embrace her for, hold the unknown against me for? To repeat the experience of self discovery. But I have discovered myself—I am not infinite. Still I can repeat the experience. But it will not be discovery. Still I can repeat the experience. —That is, I can get a sensation. The repeating of a known reaction upon myself is sensationalism. This is what nearly all English people now do. When a man takes a woman, he is merely repeating a known reaction upon himself, not seeking a new reaction, a discovery. And this is like self-abuse or masterbation. [Lawrence's spelling.—Ed.] The ordinary Englishman of the educated class goes to a woman now to masterbate himself. Because he is not going for discovery or new connection or progression, but only to repeat upon himself a known reaction.

When this condition arrives, there is always Sodomy. The man goes to the man to repeat this reaction upon himself. It is a nearer form of masterbation. But still it has some object—there are still two bodies instead of one. A man of strong soul has too

[33]

much honour for the other body—man or woman—to use it as a means of masterbation. So he remains neutral, inactive. That is Forster.

Sodomy only means that a man knows he is chained to the rock, so he will try to get the finest possible sensation out of himself.

This happens whenever the form of any living becomes too strong for the life within it: the clothes are more important than the man: therefore the man must get his satisfaction beneath the clothes.

Any man who takes a woman is up against the unknown. And a man prefers rather to have nothing to do with a woman than to have to slink away without answering the challenge. Or if he is a mean souled man, he will use the woman to masterbate himself.

There comes a point when the shell, the form of life, is a prison to the life. Then the life must either concentrate on breaking the shell, or it must turn round, turn in upon itself, and try infinite variations of a known reaction upon itself. Which produces a novelty. So that "The Rosary" is a new combination of known re-actions—so is Gilbert Cannan's "Young Earnest"—so is the cinematograph drama & all our drama & all our literature.

Or, the best thing such a life can do, that knows it is confined, is to set-to to arrange and assort all the facts & knowledge of the contained life. Which is what Plato did & what most of our writers are doing on a mean scale. They know that they are enclosed entirely by the shell, the form of living. There is no going beyond it. They are bound down.

Now either we have to break the shell, the form, the whole frame, or we have got to turn to this inward activity of setting the house in order & drawing up a list before we die.

But we shall smash the frame. The land, the industries, the means of communication & the public amusements shall all be nationalised. Every man shall have his wage till the day of his death, whether he work or not, so long as he works when he is fit. Every woman shall have her wage till the day of her death, whether she work or not, so long as she works when she is fit— keeps her house or rears her children.

Then, and then only, shall we be able to *begin* living. Then we shall be able to *begin* to work. Then we can examine marriage and love and all. Till then, we are fast within the hard, unliving, impervious shell.

You must have patience with me & understand me when my language is not clear.

I shall come and see you on the Sunday, March 7th, if you still invite me, because I want to meet Lowes Dickinson & the good people you are going to introduce me to.

It is very nice and spring-like. The birds are beginning to sing. I laugh at them. Their voices are quite rusty & stiff with a winter of disuse. The blackbird goes at it so hard, to get his whistle clear, & the wood-pigeon is so soon disheartened.

Yours sincerely

D. H. LAWRENCE

GREATHAM,

PULBOROUGH,

SUSSEX.

26 Feb. 1915

DEAR BERTRAND RUSSELL,

Your letter was very kind to me, & somehow made me feel as if I were impertinent—a bit. You have worked so hard in the abstract beyond me, I feel as if I should never be where you have been for so long, & are now—it is not my destiny. And if you are there beyond me, I feel it impertinent to talk & write so vehemently. I feel you are tolerant when you listen. Which is rather saddening. I wish you'd tell me when I am foolish & over-insistent.

I have only to stick to my vision of a life when men are freer from the immediate material things, where they need never be as they are now on the defense against each other, largely because of the struggle for existence, which is a real thing, even to those who need not make the struggle.) So a vision of a better life must include a revolution of society. And one must fulfil ones vision as much as possible. And the drama shall be between individual men & women, not between nations & classes. And the great living experience for every man is his adventure into the woman. And the ultimate passion of every man is to »realise« be within himself the whole of mankind—which I call social passion—which is what brings to fruit your philosophical writings. The

[36]

man embraces in the woman all that is not himself, and from that one resultant, from that embrace, comes every new action.

Apart from this, a man can only take that which is already known, hold it to himself, and say "this is good—or true—and this is not good, not true." But this is only the sifting or re-stating of that which is given, it is not the making of a new movement, a new combination.

I hope this doesn't sound all foolish to you.

I wrote a book about these things—I used to call it *Le Gai Savaire.* I want now to re-write this stuff, & make it as good as I can, & publish it in pamphlets, weekly or fortnightly, & so start a campaign for »my« this freer life. I want to talk about it when I come to Cambridge. I want to come—I want to come on the 6*th* & stay to the 8*th*—but are the two nights too long? I don't want you to put up with my talk, when it is foolish, because you think perhaps it is passionate. And it is not much good my asking you about your work. I should have to study it a long time first. And it is not in me. I feel quite sad, as if I talked a little vulgar language of my own which nobody understood. But if people all turn into stone or pillars of salt, one must still talk to them. You must put off your »greater« further knowledge and experience, & talk to me my way, & be with me, or I feel a babbling idiot & an intruder. My world is real, it is a true world, »& my heart knows it.« & it is a world I have in my measure understood. But no doubt you also have a true world, which I can't understand. It makes me »very« sad to conclude that. But you must live in my world, while I am there. Because it *is* also a real world. And it is a world you can inhabit with me, if I can't inhabit yours with you.

I hope I shall see Lowes Dickinson too.

D. H. LAWRENCE

GREATHAM,

PULBOROUGH,

SUSSEX.

Will you tell me if I must bring evening suit: don't bother to
write if it is *not* necessary—but a line if it is

March 2 1915

DEAR RUSSELL,

I shall come on Saturday by the train arriving Cambridge
6·2, leaving Liverpool St. 4·50. But if I can get a week-end
ticket from London, and if it obliges me to come by another
train, I will send you a post card on Friday night. I hope that
will do.

I have finished my novel so am very glad. I am also very
excited about my novel. I feel like a bird in spring that is amazed
at the colours of its own coat.

Also I feel very profound about my book "The Signal"—Le
Gai Saver—or whatever it is—which I am re-beginning. It is my
revolutionary utterance. I take on a very important attitude of
profundity to it, & so feel happy.

Also I feel frightfully important coming to Cambridge—quite
momentous the occasion is to me. I don't want to be horribly
impressed and intimidated, but am afraid I may be. I only care
about the revolution we shall have. But immediately I only want
us to be friends. But you are so shy & then I feel so clumsy, so
clownish. Don't make me see too many people at once, or I lose

my wits. I am afraid of concourses and clans and societies and cliques—not so much of individuals. Truly I am rather afraid.

Yours

D. H. LAWRENCE

GREATHAM,

PULBOROUGH,

SUSSEX.

Thank you very much for the umbrella.

Monday [March 15, 1915]

DEAR RUSSELL,

I wanted to write to you when there was something to write about: also when I could send you some of the "philosophy". But the time goes by, & I haven't done enough of the writing, & there isn't any news. I shall send you the philosophy when I have done these first crucial chapters. I cannot help being very much interested in God & the devil—particularly the devil—and in immortality. I cannot help writing about them in the "philosophy". But all the time I am struggling in the dark—very deep in the dark—and cut off from everybody & everything. Sometimes I seem to stumble into the light, for a day, or even two days— then in I plunge again, God knows where & into what utter darkness of chaos. I don't mind very much. But sometimes I am afraid of the terrible things that are real, in the darkness, and of the entire unreality of these things I see. It becomes like a madness at last, to know one is all the time walking in a pale assembly of an unreal world—this house, this furniture, the sky & the earth—whilst oneself is all the while a piece of darkness pulsating in shocks, & the shocks & the darkness are real. The whole universe of darkness & dark passions—the subterranean universe—not inferno, because that is "after"—the subterranean black universe of the things which have not yet had being—has conquered for me now, & I can't escape. So I think with fear of having to talk to anybody, because I can't talk.

But I wanted to write this to ask you please to be with me—in the underworld—or at any rate to wait for me. Don't let me go, that is all. Keep somewhere, in the darkness of reality, a connection with me. I feel there is something to go through—something very important. It may be it is only in my own soul—but it seems to grow more & more looming, & this day time reality becomes more & more unreal, as if one wrote from a grave or a womb—they are the same thing, at opposite extremes. I wish you would swear a sort of allegiance with me.

D. H. LAWRENCE

GREATHAM—PULBOROUGH—SUSSEX

Friday [March 19, 1915]

DEAR RUSSELL,

It is true Cambridge made me very black & down. I cannot bear its smell of rottenness, marsh-stagnancy. I get a melancholic malaria. How can so sick people rise up? They must die first.

I was too sad to write my "philosophy" (forgive the word) any more. I can't write it when I am depressed or hopeless. But it comes back all right, the philosophy & the belief. God help us, & give us endurance.

When will you come & see us? Don't lapse back from the promise. Remember you will come & we will have a good time—vogue la galère. Will ask Mr. Hardy if he will come & see us during vacation—I should be glad.

You know Lady Ottoline is making us a cottage at Garsington which she will lend to us. She is so generous, one shrinks a bit. One feels one would rather give things to a woman so generous. Do you think it will make an appreciable difference to her to make the cottage?—to her weight of expenses?

Do you still speak at the W.D.C. of the nations kissing each other, when your soul prowls the frontier all the time most jealously, to defend what it has & to seize what it can. It makes me laugh when you admit it. But we are all like that. Only, let us seize and defend that which is worth having, & which we want.

Saluti di cuore

D. H. LAWRENCE

GREATHAM,

PULBOROUGH,

SUSSEX.

Thrsday [sic] [April 29, 1915]

DEAR RUSSELL,

They are going to make me a bankrupt because I can't—& won't—pay the £150 of the divorce costs. I wouldn't pay them if I were a millionaire—I would rather go to prison. Messrs Goldberg Newall & Co, beasts, bugs, leeches, shall not have a penny from me if I can help it.

Today a very unclean creature came & gave me a paper, saying I must go on May 10th before the registrar & declare what debts are owing me. I'm sorry to say the publishers owe about £200, but as that is the last money I can possibly make for the next two years, they won't take it all from me.

Would you believe it, the unclean object gave me 25/, & a paper—& I had to sign the receipt "25/—for conduct money". What conduct? I am still gazing blankly at the golden sovereign. But I spat on it for luck.

I cannot tell you how this reinforces in me my utter hatred of the whole establishment—the whole constitution of England as it now stands. I wish I were a criminal instead of a bankrupt. But softly—softly. I will do my best to lay a mine under their foundations.

So we shall come to town on May 8th. I hope we shall be able to see you. I don't know where we shall stay, but I shall let you know.

Don't imagine I want any money—I don't. I wish I could tell the registrar I had n't twopence—neither in hand nor owing. But I can't, because Methuen owes me £190—to be paid when this novel is published.

I wanted to write & tell you—I don't know why. But you can't »tell« imagine how it wears on one, having at every moment to resist this established world, & to know its unconscious hostility. For I am hostile, hostile, hostile to all that is, in our public & national life. I want to destroy it.

Let us know if you will be in town next weekend but one. Herzliche—no, Freundliche Grüsse, Frieda says.

D. H. LAWRENCE

GREATHAM—PULBOROUGH—SUSSEX

29 May 1915

DEAR RUSSELL,

If they hound you out of Trinity, so much the better: I am glad. Entire separation, that is what must happen to one: not even the nominal shelter left, not even the mere fact of inclusion in the host. One must be entirely cast forth.

As for political revolution, that too must come. But now, only the darkness thrusts more & more between us all, like a sword, cutting us off entirely each from the other, severing us and burying us each one separate in the utter darkness. After this we shall know the change, we shall really move back in one movement to the sun. Except a seed die, it bringeth not forth. Only wait. Our death must be accomplished first, then we will rise up. Only wait, & be ready. We shall have to sound the resurrection soon. Leave your Cambridge then: that is very good. And let us die from this life, from this year of life, & rise up when the winter is drawing over, after the time in the tomb. But we are never dead. When everything else is gone, & there is no touch nor sense of each other left, there is always the sense of God, of the Absolute. Our sense of the Absolute is the only sense left to us.

Soon we are leaving here. You must come & see us before we go, if you can. It is beautiful. We are one in allegiance, really,

you & I. We have one faith, we must unite in one fight. Wait
only a little while—

D. H. LAWRENCE

2 June 1915

DEAR RUSSELL,

We shall be very glad to see you on June 19*th*—if we are still here. If we want to go away I shall tell you.

I shall be glad when you have strangled the invincible respectability that dogs your steps. What does it mean, really—Integer Vitae Scelerisque purus? But before what tribunal? I refuse to be judged by them. It is not for them to exculpate or to blame me. They are not my peers. Where are my peers? I acknowledge no more than five or six—not so many—in the world. But one must take care of the pack. When they hunt together they are very strong. *Never* expose yourself to the pack. Be careful of them. Be rather their secret enemy, the secret enemy, working to split up & dismember the pack from inside, not from outside. Don't make attacks from outside. Don't give yourself into their power. Don't do it.

And whoever dies, let us not die. Let us kill this hydra, this pack, before we die.

I shall be glad to see you again. I shall give you my philosophy.

Hillaire [Hilaire] Belloc says, peace in two months. All the Bellocites are convinced. I am not. I think like you, more death, & ever more death, till the fire burns itself out. Let it be so—I am willing. But I won't die. Let us remain & get a new start made, when we can get a look in.   Yrs

D. H. LAWRENCE

GREATHAM—PULBOROUGH

8 June 1915

Dear Russell,

I send you the first quarter of my philosophy. You must
n't think it bosh. I depend on you to help me with it. Don't go
against me, & say it doesn't interest you, or that there are beautiful things in it, or something like that. But help me, & tell me
where I can say the thing better.

I got the Labour Leader with your article against Lord Northcliffe. I think Lord Northcliffe wants sinking to the bottom, but
you do say rash things, & give yourself away. Let me beg you
not to get into trouble now, at this juncture. I do beg you to save
yourself for the great attack, later on, when the opportunity
comes. We must go much deeper & beyond Lord Northcliffe.
Let us wait a little while, till we can assemble the nucleus of a
new belief, get a new centre of attack, not using Labour Leaders
& so on.

We are going to Garsington Saturday—»Tuesday« Wednesday. I wonder if we shall see you there. At any rate you are
coming to us on the 19th. Then we will thresh out this business.
I wonder if you would like to meet Murry—but not this time.

D. H. Lawrence

Don't be rash now, against Northcliffes. They will fall.

GREATHAM—PULBOROUGH

Wednesday [July 6, 1915]

DEAR RUSSELL,

Are you doing the lectures. I have dropped writing my philosophy, but I go on working very hard in my soul. I shall lift up my voice in the autumn, & in connection with you, not apart. I have been wrong, much too Christian, in my philosophy. These early Greeks have clarified my soul. I must drop all about God.

You must drop all your democracy. You must not believe in "the people". One class is no better than another. It must be a case of Wisdom, or Truth. Let the working classes *be* working classes. That is the truth. There must be an aristocracy of people »of« who have wisdom, & there must be a Ruler: a Kaiser: no Presidents & democracies. I shall write out Herakleitos, on tablets of bronze.

"And it is law, too, to obey the Council of one."

"For what thought or wisdom have they? They follow the poets & take the crowd as their teacher, knowing not that there are many bad & few good. For even the best of them choose one thing above all others, immortal glory among mortals: while more of them are glutted like beasts."

"They vainly purify themselves by defiling themselves with blood."

I am sure, now, that if we go on with the war, we shall be beaten by Germany. I am sure that, unless the new spirit comes, we shall be »*badly*« irrecoverably beaten. Remember when you write your lectures, that you are a beaten nation. We are a beaten nation. It is no longer a case for satire or gibe or criticism. It is for a new »hope,« truth, a further belief.

Also we must write together, not work apart.

I am rid of all my Christian religiosity. It was only a muddiness. You need not mistrust me. In fact you don't.

In »about« a fortnight now I shall come to town.

Murry, on the Sunday, was himself again.

"If you do not expect the unexpected, you will not find it. For it is hard to sought out, and difficult."

It is only the unexpected can help us now.

D. H. Lawrence

GREATHAM,

PULBOROUGH,

SUSSEX.

Friday 15 July. [1915]

In your lecture on the State, you must criticise the extant *democracy*, the young idea. That is our enemy. This existing phase is now in its collapse. What we must hasten to prevent is this young democratic party from getting into power. The idea of giving power to the hands of the working class is *wrong*. The working man must elect the immediate government, of his »wife« work, of his »home« district, not the ultimate government of the nation. There must be a body of chosen patricians. There must be »a« woman governing equally with men, especially all the »domestic[?]« inner half of life. The whole must culminate in an absolute *Dictator*, & an equivalent *Dictatrix*. There must be none of your bourgeois presidents of Republics. The women's share must be equal with the men's. You must work this out in your own way. But you must do it.

Can't you see the whole state is collapsing. Look at the Welsh strike. This war is going to develop into the last great war between labour & capital. It will be a ghastly chaos of destruction, if it is left to Labour to be constructive. The fight must immediately be given a higher aim than the triumph of Labour, or we shall have another French Revolution. The deadly Hydra now is the hydra of Equality. Liberty, Equality & Fraternity is the

[52]

will be a ghastly chaos of destruction, if it is left to Labour to be constructive. The fight must immediately be given a higher aim than the triumph of Labour, or we shall have another French Revolution. The deadly Hydra now is the hydra of Equality. Liberty, Equality & Fraternity is the three-fanged serpent. You must have a government based upon good, better & best. You must get this into your lectures, at once. You are too old-fashioned. The basis of your serpent is already broken.

A new constructive idea of a new state is needed immediately. Criticism is unnecessary. It is behind the times. You must work out the idea of a new state, not go on criticising this old one. Get anybody & everybody to help — Orage, Shaw, anybody, but it must be a new State. And the idea is, that every man shall vote according to his understanding, & that the highest understanding must dictate for the lower understandings. And the desire is to have a perfect government perfectly related in all its parts, the highest aim of the government is the highest good of the soul, the individual, the fulfilment in the Infinite, in the Absolute. In a fortnight I shall come & take account of you D.H.L.

A page from Letter Number 11

three-fanged serpent. You must have a government based upon good, better & best. You must get this into your lectures, at once. You are too old-fashioned. The back of your serpent is already broken.

A»n« new constructive idea of a new state is needed *immedi-ately*. Criticism is *unnecessary*. It is behind the times. You *must* work out the idea of a new state, not go on criticising this old one. Get anybody & everybody to help—Orage, Shaw, anybody, but it »l[?]« must be a *new State*. And the idea is, that every man shall vote according to his »higher« understanding, & that the highest understanding must dictate for the lower understandings. And the desire is to have a perfect government perfectly related in all its parts, the highest aim of the government is the highest good of the *soul*, of the individual, the fulfilment in the Infinite, in the Absolute.

In a fortnight I shall come & take account of you

D. H. L.

GREATHAM—PULBOROUGH

26 July 1915

DEAR RUSSELL,

I rather hated your letter, & am terrified of what you are putting in your lectures. I don't want tyrants. But I don't believe in democratic control. I think the working man is fit to elect governors or overseers for his immediate circumstances, but for no more. You must utterly revise the electorate. The working man shall elect superiors for the things that concern him immediately, no more. From the other classes, as they rise, shall be elected the higher governors. The thing must culminate in one real head, as every organic thing must—no foolish republics with foolish presidents, but an elected King, something like Julius Caesar. And as the men elect & govern the industrial side of life, so the women must elect & govern the domestic side. And there must be a rising rank of women governors, as of men, culminating in a woman Dictator, of equal authority with the supreme Man. It is n't bosh, but rational sense. The whole thing must be living. Above all there must be no democratic control—that is the worst of all. There must be an elected aristocracy.

As for Horace [Horatio] Bottomley, a nation in a false system acting in a false spirit will quite rightly choose him. But a nation striving for the truth & the establishment of truth & right will forget him in a second.

I shan't come to Garsington at once, because I am not quite

in the mood. We are going on Friday to the seaside, to Little-hampton for a week. Then we go to London. Then we might arrange a meeting all together at Garsington, if Lady Ottoline can do with us.

I care only about the autumn venture—that must be a real thing.

Frieda sends her greetings

Yours

D. H. LAWRENCE

We must have the same general ideas if we are going to be or to do anything. I will listen gladly to all your ideas: but we must *put our ideas together*. This is a united effort, or it is nothing—a mere tiresome playing about, lecturing & so on. It is no mere personal voice that must be raised: but a sound, living idea round which we all rally.

1 BYRON VILLAS

   VALE OF HEALTH

      HAMPSTEAD

         N.W.

            5 Aug 1915

DEAR RUSSELL,

We are up here now for good—in the throes of furnishing. It is a great struggle. But it won't take long. When it is sufficiently done, let us go to Garsington if Lady Ottoline is free. At present I am delivered up to chairs & tables & door-mats. You might come up & see us on Saturday if you are in town. I am *very* dislocated & unhappy in these new circumstances—but shall get all right soon. We will put our heads together directly, though.

            Auf wiedersehen

              D. H. LAWRENCE

1 BYRON VILLAS — VALE OF HEALTH — HAMPSTEAD N. W.

5 Sept 1915

DEAR RUSSELL,

We are going to start a little paper, myself & Murry & Katharine Mansfield (Mrs Murry)—& you & Cannan if you care to
join. We have found a little printer in the East End, who will
print us a little booklet, leaves of the same size as the Mercure
de France, on decent paper, 36 pages of 36 lines each (about 10
words a line), 250 copies for £6: or 28 pages for £5. I think we
shall call it "The Signature"—which means a little booklet made
out of one folded leaf—also whatever else you like. At present,
we think of having 28 pages. It will be 10,000 words: that is
about 3000 words each. It will come out every fortnight, & will
be posted to subscribers. It is not for public sale (not at first, at
any rate), but we are going to get subscribers, people who care
about things, 2/6 subscription for 3 months (6 copies), postage
free. I shall be the preacher, Murry will be the revealer of the
individual soul with respect to the big questions, particularly he
will give an account of the real freedom of the individual soul,
as he conceives it; Katharine will do satirical sketches. You will
do something serious, I hope, & Gilbert can flounder prehistori-
cally.

250 half crowns are £31"5"0. That would just pay for the
6 copies of 28 pages each, & for postage.

The thing would come out the first & third Monday in every

[57]

month, beginning the first Monday in October, if possible. The printer must have the copy 15 days before publication, because he does everything himself.

I only want people who really care, & who really want a new world, to subscribe. If we lose money, it can't be very much. Murry & I will share that. At any rate we shall try the three months.

I wish, if you are in town, you would come & see us.

Yours

D. H. LAWRENCE

On "The Danger to Civilization"

BYRON VILLA — VALE OF HEALTH — HAMPSTEAD N W

14 Sept 1915

DEAR RUSSELL,

I'm going to quarrel with you again. You simply don't speak the truth, you simply are not sincere. The article you send me is a plausible lie, and I hate it. If it says some true things, that is not the point. The fact is that you, in the Essay, are all the time a lie.

Your basic desire is the maximum of desire of war, you are really the super-war-spirit. What you want is to jab and strike, like the soldier with the bayonet, only you are sublimated into words. And you are like a soldier who might jab»s« man after man with his bayonet, saying "this is for ultimate peace." The soldier »is« would be a liar. And it isn't in the least true that you, your basic self, want ultimate peace. You are satisfying in an indirect, false way your lust to jab and strike. Either satisfy it in a direct and honorable way, saying "I hate you all, liars and swine, and am out to set upon you", or stick to mathematics, where you can be true—But to come as the angel of peace—no, I prefer Tirpitz a thousand times in that rôle.

You are simply *full* of repressed desires, which have become savage and anti-social. And they come out in this sheep's clothing of peace propaganda. As a woman said to me, who had been to one of your meetings: "It seemed so strange, with his face looking so evil, to be talking about peace and love. He can't have 'meant what he said."

I believe in your inherent power for realising the truth. But I don't believe in your will, not for a second. Your will is false and »dark« cruel. You are too full of devilish repressions to be anything but lustful and cruel. I would rather have the German soldiers with rapine and cruelty, than you with your words of goodness. It is the falsity I can't bear. I would n't care if you were six times a murderer, so long as you said to yourself, "I am this." The enemy of all mankind, you are, full of the lust of enmity. It is *not* the hatred of falsehood which inspires you. It is the hatred of people, »all people« of flesh and blood. It is a perverted, mental blood-lust. Why don't you own it.

Let us become strangers again, I think it is better.

D. H. LAWRENCE

1, BYRON VILLAS,

VALE-OF-HEALTH,

HAMPSTEAD,

LONDON.

17 Nov. 1915

DEAR RUSSELL,

I am sorry we have promised to go out to dinner on Thursday. Could you come on Friday to tea, if you wish to leave town in the afternoon. Lady Ottoline is coming I think to lunch.

Also I may have to stay in England a little longer, to fight for my novel. Yesterday I heard from the Authors Society that they will *probably* stand by me, because the book was condemned wholly without reference to me. I don't want to stay, because now we are ready, quite ready, to go. But if I must stay to fight about the book, I will stay.

But you will come on Friday to see us. I shall be very glad to talk to you again, to be friends. After all, my quarrelling with you was largely a quarrelling with something in *myself*, something I was struggling away from in myself.

Yours

D. H. LAWRENCE

Dec. [6] 1915

1, BYRON VILLAS,

VALE-OF-HEALTH,

HAMPSTEAD,

LONDON.

Monday

DEAR RUSSELL,

We want to go away to America, soon—on the 24*th* of this month, if possible. Will you come up & see us one day this week—Friday evening perhaps? I should be glad to see you before we go: so would Frieda. We are not really enemies: it is only a question of attitude.

I send you your book. Thank you very much for lending it me. Do come and see us one day this week.

Yours

D. H. LAWRENCE

1 BYRON VILLAS — VALE OF HEALTH — HAMPSTEAD N. W.

8 Dec. 1915

DEAR RUSSELL,

I called to see you yesterday but you were out. I hope you will come up and see us soon. —No definite developement in our plans.

I have been reading Frazer's Golden Bough and Totemism & Exogamy. Now I am convinced of what I believed when I was about twenty—that there is another seat of consciousness than the brain & the nerve system: there is a blood-consciousness which exists in us independently of the ordinary mental consciousness, which depends on the eye as its source or connector. There is the blood-consciousness, with the sexual connection holding the same relation as the eye, in seeing, holds to the mental consciousness. One lives, knows, and has one's being in the blood, without any reference to nerves and brain. This is one half of life, belonging to the darkness. And the tragedy of this our life, and of your life, is that the mental and nerve consciousness exerts a tyranny over the blood-consciousness and that your will has gone completely over to the mental consciousness, and is engaged in the destruction of your blood-being or blood-consciousness, the final liberating of the one, which is only death in result. Plato was the same. Now it is necessary for us to realise that there is this other great half of our life active in the darkness, the blood-relationship: that when I *see*, there is a connection between my mental-consciousness and an outside body, forming a percept; but at the same time, there is a transmission through the darkness which is never absent from the light, into my blood-consciousness: but in seeing, the blood-percept is perhaps not strong. On the other hand, when I take a woman, then the blood-percept is supreme, my blood-knowing is overwhelming. There is a transmission, I don't know of what, between her blood & mine, in the act of connection. So that afterwards, even if she goes away, the blood-consciousness persists between us, when the mental consciousness is suspended; and I am formed then by my blood-consciousness, not by my mind or nerves at all.

Similarly in the transmission from the blood of the mother to the embryo in the womb, there goes the whole blood consciousness. And when they say a mental image is sometimes transmitted from the mother to the embryo, this is not the *mental* image, but the *blood-image*. All living things, even plants, have a blood-being. If a lizard falls on the breast of a pregnant woman, then the blood-being of the lizard passes with a shock into the blood-being of the woman, and is transferred to the foetus, probably without intervention either of nerve or brain consciousness. And this is the origin of totem: and for this reason some tribes no doubt really *were* kangaroos: they contained the blood-knowledge of the kangaroo.—And blood knowledge comes either through the mother or through the sex—so that

[64]

dreams at puberty are as good an origin of the totem as the percept of a pregnant woman.

This is very important to our living, that we should realise
that we have a blood-being, a blood-consciousness, a blood-soul,
complete and apart from the mental & nerve consciousness.

Do you know what science says about these things? It is *very*
important: the whole of our future life depends on it.

Yours

D. H. LAWRENCE

Wednesday [December 22-23 [?], 1915]

DEAR RUSSELL,

I got your letter this morning: thank you for the £2. We sent the reproductions to Lady Ottoline—they were *really beautiful*. But I haven't had the bill yet: I will straighten up with you when it comes.

We go to Cornwall on Thursday—30*th*. The address is c/o J D Beresford, Porthcothan St. Merryn, Padstow, Cornwall. Come and see us there—& stay a week or so. Don't be so despondent about your lectures.

We are waiting to go to Florida, for the others. We must go as a little body: it is not a personal matter—it is a bigger thing. There are several young people very anxious to come. I must wait for them. I can't go without them. We shall be six or seven. As soon as they are free to come, then we shall sail off. It is all so complicated, because of money & the war. They are all very young people. We can go & start a new life in a new spirit—a spirit of coming together, not going apart. Won't you come to Florida too? Do! It is hopeless to stay in England. Do you come & be president of us.

It is so queer being up here at home. The colliers are queer too. I wish you were here to have a talk. But more & more I realise it is hopeless to stay in England.

Greetings from Frieda & me   D. H. LAWRENCE

Thank you for sending the ticket to Barbara Low.

PORTHCOTHAN,

ST MERRYN,

NORTH CORNWALL.

13 Jan 1916.

DEAR BERTIE,

I have never written to you all the while we have been here, and I've thought about you nearly every day, wondering & wondering what you are doing and how you are feeling; how the lectures are now, & when you begin them, and how you feel about them. Do write and let me know.

I owe you some money. We got those frescoes for 3 guineas. That is, your share, 31/6. Therefore I owe you 8/6. I will send it you, I won't forget.

I like being here *very much*. Cornwall isn't England. It isn't really England, nor Christendom. It has another quality: of King Arthur's days, that flicker of Celtic consciousness before it was swamped under Norman and Teutonic waves. I like it very much. I like the people also. They've got a curious softness, and intimacy. I think they've lived from just the opposite principle to Christianity: self-fulfilment and social destruction, instead of social love & self-sacrifice. So here there is no social structure, hardly, & the people have hardly any social self: only the immediate intimate self. That's why they're generally disliked. And that's why they were wreckers & smugglers & all antisocial things. And that's why the roads are too dodgy to be grasped.

And that's why there is such a lovely intimate softness in the women.

I have suddenly launched off into my philosophy again. Now this time I have got it—my heart is satisfied. I don't want to polish it up, I am so pleased with it. I shall send it you when it is done & typed out, and you must read it with pleasure.

At present Heseltine and Kouzoumdjian are here. I don't know how long they will stay. It is a wee bit painful—these young individualists are so disintegrated: *are* the young more sound than the old? It seems to me they are much more sick.

We've got a jolly old farmhouse, & a good housekeeper. I wish you could come & see us. Come & stay, when your lectures are over, will you. Do come. We shall be here I think till the middle of March—then where, I dont know.

We are just on the sea, looking down into a little cove. The water smashes up the black rocks. It is nice. Then the bare, unformed, uhrzeitig landscape—there really might be rock-hurling giants & odd pixies. If only it were n't all cut up into fields! If only the Cornish had n't become foully and uglily Wesleyan. Alas alas!

What is going to become of the world? I wish we were off to Florida. The desert is the only place.

Frieda sends her love, I mine.

Yours

D. H. LAWRENCE

Write & tell me how things are with you

[68]

PORTHCOTHAN — ST. MERRYN — NORTH CORNWALL

11 Feb. 1916

MY DEAR RUSSELL,

I have been thinking about you and your lectures. Are they really a success, & really vital? Are you really glad?—or only excited? I want to know, truly.

I have been very seedy down here—really felt as if I should die—but now am getting better quickly.

What a bitter thing it is, to feel swamped right over by these seas of utter falsehood. One does really die. But one is not dead.

I have been thinking, the only idea is to found a publishing company, that publishes for the sake of the truth. That is the only way. The spoken word nowadays is almost bound to be a lie: because the collective listening ear is a lie. I could never speak truth to 20 collected people.

We must send round circulars for our publishing: begin with The Rainbow: publish it at 7/6, by subscription. When we have a sufficient number of names to justify us, we could begin. Then we could go on, print every other month a *real* book, if a real book came. If no real book came, then we would wait till it did. A book is a holy thing, & must be made so again.

Tell me how you are, & how things are with you, & if you agree about the publishing concern.

Yours

D. H. LAWRENCE

[PORTHCOTHAN, ST MERRYN, CORNWALL]

Saturday [February 19, 1916]

MY DEAR RUSSELL,

I did n't like your letter. What's the good of living as you do, anyway. I don't believe your lectures *are* good. They are nearly over, are n't they?

What's the good of sticking in the damned ship and haranguing the merchant-pilgrims in their own language. Why don't you drop overboard? Why don't you clear out of the whole show?

One must be an outlaw these days, not a teacher or preacher. One must retire out of the herd & then fire bombs into it. You said in your lecture on education that you did n't set much count by the unconscious. That is sheer perversity. The whole of the consciousness and the conscious content is old hat—the millstone round your neck.

Do cut it—cut your will and leave your old self behind. Even your mathematics are only *dead* truth: and no matter how fine you grind the dead meat, you'll not bring it to life again.

Do stop working & writing altogether and become a creature instead of a mechanical instrument. Do clear out of the whole social ship. Do for your very pride's sake become a mere nothing, a mole, a creature that feels its way & does n't think. Do for heavens sake be a baby, & not a savant any more. Don't *do* anything any more—but for heavens sake begin to *be*—start at

[70]

the very beginning and be a perfect baby: in the name of courage.

Oh, and I want to ask you, when you make your will, do leave me enough to live on. I want you to live for ever. But I want you to make me in some part your heir.

We have got to clear out of this house in a week's time. We are looking for another house. You had better come & live near us: but not if you are going to be a thinker and a worker, only if you are going to be a creature, an infant. The Murrys are coming to live with us in April, they say.

Heseltine is starting the publishing scheme. I should n't wonder if he would make something of it, if he is n't conscripted. I feel as if we were all living on the edge of a precipice. Soon I shall be penniless, & they'll shove me into munitions, & I shall tell 'em what I think of 'em, & end my days in prison or a madhouse. But I don't care. One can still write bombs. But I don't want to be penniless and at their mercy. Life is very good of itself, and I am terrified lest they should get me into their power. They seem to me like an innumerable host of rats, & once they get the scent, one is lost.

My love to you. Stop working and being an ego, & have the courage to be a creature.

Yours

D. H. LAWRENCE

TINNERS ARMS,   ZENNOR,   ST. IVES, CORNWALL.

9 March 1916

MY DEAR RUSSELL,

Are you still cross with me for being a schoolmaster & for not respecting the rights of man? Don't be, it isn't worth it.

Your lectures are over, are they? What are you going to do now?

We have taken a tiny cottage here, for £5 a year, which we shall furnish. We shall live very cheaply, because we are going to be very poor indeed. But just under the wild hills with their great grey boulders of granite, and above the big sea, it is beautiful enough, & free enough. I think we can be obscure, and happy, like creatures in a cave.

You must come down to Cornwall some time and have rooms in a farm-house. Will you do that?

One must learn to be happy & careless. The old world never tumbles down except a young world shoves it over, heedlessly. And I'm sure the young world must be jolly. So let us have a good time to ourselves while the old world tumbles over itself. It is no good bothering. Nothing is born by taking thought. That which is born comes of itself. All we can do is to refrain from frustrating the new world which »from« is being born in us.

At the present we only think of getting into our tiny cottage—furnishing, & so on. Later we can dance with the springtime, very soon.

I hope we shall see you before long.

Yours

D. H. LAWRENCE

LAWRENCE'S CORRECTIONS ON RUSSELL'S MANUSCRIPT

The following material is the lecture outline Russell sent Lawrence early in July of 1915, prefaced by Lawrence's criticism of it. Russell's manuscript is full of Lawrence's marginal and interlinear disagreements, superimposed on Russell's typescript. These are here printed in square brackets and in italics. Words of Russell that Lawrence crossed out are enclosed in French quotation marks » «; so are corrections of his own remarks. These last are as well in italics and in square brackets. Lawrence's comments are written across Russell's manuscript so wildly that they make exact typographic reproduction impossible, as the facsimile facing p. 88 demonstrates.

LAWRENCE'S CORRECTIONS ON
RUSSELL'S MANUSCRIPT

Don't be angry that I have scribbled all over your work. But this which you say is all social criticism: it isn't social reconstruction. You must take a plunge into another element if it is to be social reconstruction.

Primarily, you must allow and acknowledge & be prepared to proceed from the fundamental impulse in all of us towards The Truth, the fundamental passion also, the most fundamental passion in man, for Wholeness of Movement, Unanimity of Purpose, Oneness in Construction. This is the principle of Construction. The rest is all criticism, destruction.

Do, do get these essays ready, for the love of God. But make them more profound, more philosophical. Make them not popular, oh, not popular »A great idea is «. The best is to attack the spirit, then proceed to the form. You call the spirit Subjectivism. Do go to the root of this: kill it at the root. Show how everything works upon this great falsity of subjectivism, now. I like it where

[77]

you take them one by one, The State, Marriage, etc. But you must put in the positive idea. Every living community is a living State. You must go very deep into the State, & its relation to the individual.

We shall be at 32 Well Walk, Hampstead—Mrs. Radford—this week-end. I must see you.

Above all don't be angry with my scribbling. But above all, do do these lectures.

I must lecture—or preach—on religion—give myself away.

But you must dare very much more than you have done here —you must dare be positive, not only critical.

D. H. LAWRENCE

PHILOSOPHY OF
SOCIAL RECONSTRUCTION

I. The disease: disintegration. The remedy: cooperation, not authority.

II. The old cohesions: The State, Property, The Churches, Law and Morality, Marriage. All based on Power, not on Liberty and Love. All want fundamental reconstruction.

III. Subjectivism: growth of hard Ego in fight for liberty. Luther; philosophy. Two forms of subjectivism: *my* dominion, *my* dominion, *my* sensations. Hence imperialism and decadent vice. No love, but enjoyment of absorbing another ego, or of sensation of love.

IV. War: primitive impulse to war only very partially concerned in this war. Need of excitement; weariness; disillusionment; impulse to suicide. This war not for any object, but subjective; will stop when people are tired of it.

V. Industrialism: divorce from satisfaction of creative impulse through capitalism. Need of economic as well as political democracy: syndicalism. Material goods not main need. No use in wealth if *ennui* remains.

VI. Life made whole: by freedom for impulse of growth and creation, by freedom to love. To be achieved by new standards, less belief in material goods, then by unity in freedom through new political institutions. No use reviving what is dead, or keeping alive what is moribund.

[Cause of Disintegration: The belief that we cannot know any fulfilment save what is allowed by our Civilised System. So our impulse towards truth & unanimity is prevented, each man acts as if he were in a cage, isolated, beyond good & evil. In this state there is only sensational experience left.]

I. FORMS OF DISINTEGRATION.

Chéradame's "La Crise Française". His cure: boy scouts.

Living for sensation: involves loneliness, prevents sense of fulfilment, leads on to perpetually stronger sensations because it has no attainable goal: ends in cruelty and Sadism.

One »great source« [»form« example]: prevention of children; turns thoughts to momentary sensation, isolates act.

[Prevention of children is only a result of disintegration—We prevent children because we want individual power (money). The act is isolated in us beforehand. The prevention is only a following out of what is. Don't dwell on children so much.]

Another source: living in towns, away from earth.

[We live in towns from choice, when we subscribe to our great civilised form. The nostalgia for the country is not so important. What is important is that our towns are false towns—every street a blow, every corner a stab.]

Another source: in men, specialising of activities; in well-to-do women, »freedom from house-work and nursing« children. *[lack of any importance whatever, save sensational effect]*

[Another example]

Observation of self: result of mental progress.

Most of these things can't be prevented: must be absorbed by some sanative purpose.

What is wanted is a direct »interest in other people« [no— no—] of a kind which develops their life and one's own at once. [*What is wanted is a knowledge of the true conditions we all desire in our souls, putting aside the fetish of what is. What is wanted is a conception of a »true« "unanimous" society. We want to create a new* Whole: *that is our fundamental desire*] In the past, marriage and the family were the great example of this. Now both have ceased to be. Husband and wife are an obstacle to each other's development; so are parents and children. This is due to a »hardening of the Ego,« [*disbelief in the principle on which marriage is founded.*] leading us to view others as means or hindrances to self-realization. In the struggle for freedom, there is a »decay of frank interest« in others. No self worth realizing is possible without a direct feeling about others. Subjectivism makes the self shrivel. But slavery also is bad. We want a life which will keep alive the frank interest »in others which one sees in dogs for example«, and we want institutions which will make this possible without subjecting either or both to slavery.

[*No no no, don't talk about interest in others. What you mean is the unanimous impulse, the impulse towards a unanimous movement. It isn't the others we are interested in, it is the* Whole,

[81]

the Whole of Us. We want to make a Whole Movement, Unanimous.]

II. (1) »THE STATE.« *[What State? There are all kinds of States. Ours is one of the strongest States in the world] [There are 2 conceptions of the State now: 1. Monarchy 2. Democracy. Democracy is the falser.]*

Still strong in Germany and Japan, not elsewhere. Depends on tribal feeling and allegiance to monarch. *[every man's having his supreme ideal in Kingship, in conceiving the King to be the most Godlike man.]* Both decaying. Two enemies, individualism and cosmopolitanism. Why serve other people in same State more than foreigners? Only fear now holds State together. *[There must be a State, & a government.]* "High treason" has a mediaeval flavour. Can't *worship* the State. *[What can I worship?]* I feel more allegiance to mathematics than to the State. *[Why?]* Syndicalism. French Revolution. Ulster State depends on war for its strength. If wars were to cease, States would dissolve.

The State is absurd »because« *[when]* it is geographical. A man ought to belong to many groups *[a high idea of the truth]*, chosen by himself, each with its own government, with only certain federal powers reserved to the geographical state, and things like water-supply, which are by nature geographical. Syndicalism.

The *[existing]* State has two functions: internal peace and external war, police and armaments, security within and insecurity without. In so far as State performs economic services, it does only what could be done otherwise. Its essence is the suppression of violence within its borders and its promotion elsewhere. It involves an entirely artificial division of mankind and of our duties towards them: towards one group we are bound by the law, towards the rest only by the prudence of highwaymen. This is absurd: external and internal anarchy both right or both wrong. Present plan supported (a) because others do it, and it is thought the only road to safety (b) because it secures the pleasures of triumph, dominion and cruelty. These pleasures are native to man, and yet cannot be obtained in a good community. Our Utopia must endeavour to compensate in other ways for the obstacles to inflicting pain.

[*You must advance on to the* New State, *where none of our sense of Truth is violated. You must* »imagine« *give some conception of it, & your perfect belief in it*]

Strength in »the« [this] State is like discipline on a pirate ship. The State [as it stands] is in its very essence an evil thing, by its exclusions, and by the fact that it is a combination of men for murder and robbery.

[*The state is the expression of a great metaphysical conception: the conception of God the Creator, who created the earth according to certain Laws, which, if obeyed, would give happiness.*]

[*We proceed to create our State according to our religious*] *belief, our philosophical conception of life. The King represents God. The Ministers subject to the King are the Archangels subject to God.*

[The metaphysical belief is no longer held. Therefore our State is a falsity.

[The State must represent the deepest philosophical or religious belief.

[What do we believe in—God the Creator? or the Son of Man?—Kingship or brotherhood, Monarchy or democracy?—neither.]

II. (2) PROPERTY.

Present laws of property quite artificial. Represent power of sword (rent) and family pride (inheritance). Should readjust law of property with reference to human happiness. Great wealth and great poverty are absurd. Inheritance is absurd. Equality would be a mistake. Object should be to provide every one as far as possible with (1) an occupation which leaves him a human being, (2) such a degree of wealth as makes possible the life suited to his occupation. No need of long hours. Wealth beyond a point ought to be illegal. Land ought to be national. Honour and success ought not to be measured by income. Increase in productivity through machines is good, but now we are slaves of machines through belief in wealth, which makes us work as hard as if there were no machines.

[The belief in wealth is »every«thing: go for that: the State

»is« now »established« rests on a belief in wealth. It is a rotten belief to hold a great Community together.]

II. (3) THE CHURCHES.

Religion, in some form, seems necessary to a good society or a good individual life. By "religion" I mean devotion to an end outside the individual life, and even, in some sense, outside human life—like God or truth or art. But the Churches consist of certain property only given to those who profess certain beliefs, now known to be false by all who think independently. Because freedom leads to rejection of these beliefs, churches oppose freedom, and like all forms of unreason—e.g. patriotism and loyalty to sovereigns. In thought, they substitute sentiment for observation, and so encourage subjectivism, which is the root of the trouble. Religion wants as much transformation as marriage and property.

Men of science have some elements of a possible new religion. They are the happiest of intelligent men.

[There is no living society possible but one which is held together by a great religious idea. We only need not be subjectively religious. But one & all we must act from a profound religious belief—not »human« individual.

[If you don't want to assert any religious belief, then criticise the false church. But it all rests on the Christian Metaphysic, which each man severally rejects, but to which we all subscribe as a State or Society]

[85]

II. (4) LAW AND MORALITY.

Law in origin religious. Decalogue and Koran. Lingers in marriage law: divorce against law of God, therefore only the rich can have it. No respect for law now. *[because the Metaphysic on which it is established is no longer held.]* We know law is human, we know it is not made in the general interest, we know it gets improved by being broken. We no longer feel horror of the criminal. All who are rich enough habitually break the law.

Morality is disapproval of community for those who act against the holders of power. Hence enemies in war are wicked by definition. Morality »is« *[has become]* essentially part of the criminal law: it is a means of bringing self-interest into harmony with the interests of others. *[There is a good morality. Morality is, when it is real, »is« the sense of truth. You must put the positive side forward, if you are going to oust the old evil.]* But when this is seen, it loses efficacy, since it depends on belief in absolute "wickedness". Certain interests uphold it: (1) that it supports those in possession, since aggression is wicked, (2) that it provides an excuse for hatred and punishment, which are pleasures, (3) that it gives occasion for self-esteem, since we ourselves are very virtuous.

Something more positive than morality must take its place, since morality is dissolved by thought. *[This is so vague. One must only know that morality is one's inviolable sense of truth.]*

What shall we do about criminal *law*? E.g. if people ill-treat their children? If men belong to voluntary groups formed by common purposes, in most cases expulsion from such groups would be sufficient penalty; consider what pains are taken to avoid open adultery, because it involves expulsion from Clubs. If people ill-treat their children, the children must be taken away, and the people made to pay for the expense, not by way of penalty, but by way of contracts for other benefits. This will probably effect all that punishment would effect.

How about burglars? In a decent community, the penalties against cheating at cards would be quite sufficient, unless a community of burglars existed. In that case, stricter measures of boycott might be necessary. But the burglars should be treated as we treat an enemy state, given every chance to make a treaty of peace, or to surrender individually, and not punished if they do not persist in burglary.

Men whose purposes clash with those of most of the community, like maniacs and congenital criminals, must be restrained in the general interest. We can not have an absolute principle against force, but we must look out for ways of minimizing its employment.

[Let the law be established on the sense of truth, & then you can use force. Because the truth is greater than any one of us. But the truth is a growing organism—or our conception of it is.]

What is essence of *morality*? *[The sense of Truth (you must say it—or something like it.)]* A man's acts affect others *[NO! NO!]* therefore others are interested in what he does. A *moral* act is one comformable to the desires of the others affected by the act. Why should a man be moral? *[Why do you use "moral" when you only mean "well-behaved")]* Because action against the desires of others makes him disliked, which is disagreeable to him. *[NO! NO! NO! NO! NO!]* But this kind of morality has a very limited efficacy: *1st*, it does not apply to large groups, like states, for the fact that Germans hate us is not disagreeable to us; *2nd*, if "immoral" impulses exist, they will often be strong enough to conquer self-interest and fear of being disliked.

The problem for the statesman should be to find out that kind of organisation and education which will prevent *[which will educate the sense of »right and« truth & justice, & train us all to act from this supreme impulse.]* "immoral" *impulses*, rather than one which merely punishes the indulgence of them. "Immoral" impulses are of »two kinds: (1) merely demanding more than one's share of personal goods, (2) positive cruelty, envy, love of power, etc.« *[one kind: the acting from the sense of the human Self, instead of from the sense of Truth. The Fabians are immoral.]* The first of these is easily regulated by institutions and appeal to justice. *[This is not good]* The second is almost always the result of a life in which some vital instinct is balked; it grows out of celibacy, military discipline, slavery, etc. and can be cured by giving a free life to everyone. It will then remain only in cripples, hunchbacks, etc.

[88]

Law and Morality (Cont.)

The sense of Truth (you must say it - or something like it.)

What is essence of morality? A man's acts affect others therefore others are interested in what he does. A moral act is one conformable to the desires of the others affected by the act. Why should a man be moral? Because action against the desires of others makes him disliked, which is disagreeable to him. But this kind of morality has a very limited efficacy: 1st, it does not apply to large groups, like states, for the fact that Germans hate us is not disagreeable to us; 2nd, if "immoral" impulses exist, they will often be strong enough to conquer self-interest and fear of being disliked.

Why do you use "moral" when you only mean "well-behaved"?

No! no! no! no!

The problem for the statesman should be to find out that kind of organisation and education which will prevent "immoral" impulses, rather than one which merely punishes the indulgence of them. "Immoral" impulses are of two kinds: (1) merely demanding more than one's share of personal goods, (2) positive cruelty, envy, love of power, etc. The first of these is easily regulated by institutions and appeal to justice. The second is almost always the result of a life in which some vital instinct is balked; it grows out of celibacy, military discipline, slavery, etc. and can be cured by giving a free life to everyone. It will then remain

Which will educate the sense of right and truth & justice, & train us all to act from this supreme impulse.

one kind: the acting from the sense of the human self, instead of from the sense of truth. The Fabians are immoral

No! no! Good!

A page from Russell's manuscript showing Lawrence's corrections

Justice and liberty are what remains of morality. These the statesman must respect.

The principle of *Tao*. Growing like a tree. The principle of growth in a man must not be crushed. It is not crushed necessarily by preventing a man from doing some definite thing, but it is often crushed by forcing him to do something else. A man who cannot marry the woman he loves may come to love someone else, but a man who marries a woman he does not love loses something of the instinctive life that makes growth. So a man need not adopt the profession he would choose, if some other similar profession is open to him; but if he has to adopt a profession repugnant to his instinct, his soul suffers. In a good community, Napoleon could not have been allowed the profession of his choice, but he might have found happiness as a pioneer in Western America. He could not have found happiness as a city clerk.

[And what is the principle of growth: is it not the prescience of conscience that which is »needed« to be, in the grown tissue is all the ungrown tissue of all time: this ungrown tissue knows its own »laws« relations . . this knowledge in us I call the sense of truth. But it is as real, much realer, than all the tangible or obvious impulses we talk of.]

II. (5) MARRIAGE.

»Resultant of sex instinct plus jealousy.« *[No!]* Depended for success on husband's authority, admitted as a right by wife.

[89]

He free, she willing slave. This was possible. Mutual liberty now demanded, makes old form of marriage impossible. Fight for liberty by women prevents both them and men from getting satisfaction in marriage. Women want to preserve their individuality; this makes union impossible. Relations become trivial and temporary, a pleasure, not a satisfaction, an excitement, not an attainment. The old tight family can't be revived. It depended on beliefs now known to be false. Seriousness in sex relations must be restored otherwise. At present, children only in marriage, not in other unions. This one source of harm. Sex relations bad without love, also without children. At present institutions prevent either love or else children in most relations.

Successful monogamy [now] depends upon the successful substitution of habit for emotion »in the course« of years. [No!] A character which does not readily form habits, or does not find habits an adequate safeguard against emotion, is not suited to monogamy. [The desire for monogamy is profound in us. But the most difficult thing in the world is to find a mate. It is still true, that a man & wife are one flesh. A man alone is only fragmentary—also a woman. Completeness is in marriage. But State-marriage is a lie.] No one who is alive will wish to be the slave of habit, or to lose the capacity for emotion. For this reason, monogamy now often harmful. Sex-relations without a common life are bad: (1) they emphasise sex too much, (2) they are exciting and disturbing, (3) they cannot bring satsifaction of instinct. But the common life need not last a lifetime. To most men, the intention of children, and its realization, are essential to satisfaction, but not the constant companionship of the children. Children ought to be left with the mother when a marriage breaks up, except in exceptional cases.

A sex-relation entered into by either side for other than sexual reasons—e.g. money—is vile; this applies to prostitution and most marriages. It degrades both man and woman, since it involves lack of reverence. Any relation which aims merely at pleasure fails to bring satisfaction. We ought to remove all obstacles to the combination of love, children, and a common life, which constitutes a good marriage. This involves opposition to monogamy and prostitution, but some tolerance of light relations as experiments.

II. SUMMARY.

All these institutions are based on Power, Power of the King, »of the husband, of the feudal baron, of God.« [»a false« an obsolete metaphysic] Since we no longer believe in Power, all live on only by inertia, and all are decaying. Hence hypocrisy. Institutions are based on the relation of Master and Slave, where the master lived a free life, and the slave had the "duty" of ministering to him. Such "duty" as we can now have must be not towards a master, but towards an ideal, and it must be of the nature of love for an ideal. The relations of human beings should be based on mutual liberty, with Love. Political institutions so based would be quite different from ours.

[91]

III. SUBJECTIVISM.

The hardening and separation of the individual. In the Roman Empire, fully developed in Stoicism, which made *my* virtue the end of life. Mediaeval Empire and Church swept away the individual. Luther began to revive him. In philosophy German idealism and English sensationalism did the same.*[do develop this!]* Two sides of subjectivism, *will* and *sensation,* one leads to militarism, the other to decadent vice. But the Wille zur Macht is less finished subjectivism than the other, since power demands an Other over whom we have power. Hence it belongs to a less developed stage than sensationalism. Now-a-days, what people enjoy when they fall in love is not the beloved object, but the "experience", their own emotion. And when a young woman first becomes a mother, every one begs her to analyse the experience. Hence no important relation results. Hence universal solitude.

[I think this is best.]

IV. WAR.

There have been wars for important objects. This not one of them.

Why men like the war: (only those who stay at home count those who go have no voice) because it relieves tedium; because it is a contest calling out primitive passions normally unexercised; because ordinary life is unsatisfying and tame; because triumph (which is expected) is delightful; because discomfort

[92]

makes men look for some one to hate; because there is a lust of destruction, including self-destruction; because in war men realize the magnitude of their State, which is a source of pride.

Modern weariness like that of late Roman Empire.

No nation is fighting for any tangible object, but because it pleases them to fight. Gradually weariness is replacing love of violence, and bringing peace.

To prevent wars, men must not be balked in their instincts, since this leads to cruelty; they must have opportunities of showing manhood and running risks. *[This too is good]*

V. INDUSTRIALISM.

[The key to this is the falsity of having for an aim the production of wealth. Our aim should be the establishment of Truth.]

Many evils in it at present, but we can't go back to condition before. Machinery and large economic organizations are unavoidable.

Evils: Life in town divorces men from instinctive satisfactions, such as smell of earth and sight of green fields. Exciting pleasures take place of satisfactions. This applies to the rich and the poor alike. Vastness of organizations and concentration in hands of capitalists, prevents employees from feeling any *pride* in their work. There is no result in which they can feel the satisfaction of the creator. A railway porter who has a little garden will work in his garden with a joy he never can feel in working for a railway company. Much industrial work is mechanical and monoto-

. nous. Even the work of directors of industry has no tangible object—it aims merely at wealth, which is an indefinite and always receding goal—it is not like artistic creation, perpetually reaching some achievement, and it is divorced from the material of the work. There is no use in merely more money. Miners earn good wages but are too uncivilized to enjoy them. No use in shorter hours, unless accompanied with means of rational enjoyment, and with education. No use abolishing poverty if *ennui* remains.

Palliations: education, shorter hours, everybody have a garden, etc.

»Root of evil« *[Re-construction]:* that those employed have no voice in directing the business. Syndicalism suggests cure. Democracy should be economic as well as political. Democracy gives sense of self-direction in enterprises which require cooperation. Railway-men should elect station-masters, station-masters should elect directors. Then a man could take a pride in his railway, and think out its problems. The staff of a newspaper ought to decide its policy. No good having the State the sole employer. The State is too big and remote; it does not give a man the sense of directing his own work.

VI. LIFE MADE WHOLE.

Most men now believe that material goods make happiness; even socialists imagine that with better wages working men would be happy. Yet the rich are not happy. People need a certain modicum of goods for happiness but this not the main need.

Some men can be happy through religion, but they are few. [*This is subjective religion. But unless the religious idea be living & extant, no one is happy.*]

Most men need two things: love leading to children, and work which gives an outlet to their creative impulse.

Most women need freedom in love, and secure possession of children.

In modern world children avoided for the sake of freedom, pride in work prevented by capitalism. If the lives of men and women were more satisfying, there would be less envy, hatred, cruelty, love of dominion, desire seeking titillations rather than satisfactions.

No use reviving what is dead, or keeping alive what is moribund.

Must free our souls, live in vision, make better world vivid to our imaginations. Must achieve a new marriage of instinct and way of life, by less belief in material goods, by new political institutions giving unity of freedom. No need of hate or conflict: only the failure of inward joy brings them about. [*There will always be hate & conflict. It is a principle of growth: every bud must burst its cover, & the cover doesn't want to be burst. But let our hatred & conflict be really part of our vital growth, the outcome of our growing, not of our desire for sensation.*] We first must get joy through religion, through spiritual freedom; then we can give it to others and bring about a happier life.

[95]

There is in men something that may be called the principle of growth—in old-fashioned language, the Soul—which is injured in industrialism. Take professions: a man becomes a journalist, and has to write for a paper whose politics he dislikes. This kills his pride in work, his sense of independence, and makes him cynical, mentally sterile or even devastating. A man becomes a doctor: if he is a general practitioner he has to fall in with humbug; if a specialist, he has to marry a heiress. In either case, his integrity is gone. A man becomes a politician: he not only has to swallow the Party programme, but he has to pretend to be a saint, to conciliate religious supporters; no man can enter Parliament without hypocrisy. Parsons have to tell lies in the most solemn way in order to get ordained. In most continental countries, learned men in youth have to profess agreement with their professors before they can get a start. In America they have to go for quick results rather than slow solid work. In no profession is there any respect for the native pride without which a man cannot remain whole; the world ruthlessly crushes it out, because it implies independence, and men desire to enslave others more than they desire to be free themselves. Inward freedom is infinitely precious: we must create a society which preserves it.

APPENDIX B

A NOTE ON THE CHRONOLOGY OF THE LETTERS

A NOTE ON THE CHRONOLOGY
OF THE LETTERS

AT THE TIME of his correspondence with Bertrand Russell, Lawrence often dated his letters with the "London, Wednesday" kind of notation. This is noticeable in the Huxley collection,* which has many of the letters through this period (particularly some of those to Lady Ottoline Morrell) placed only by guesswork. Aldous Huxley was a shrewd guesser and in the main was skillful at working out the position of various undated letters from internal evidence. Most of the mistakes he made were due to lack of corroborative material, such as the correspondence in the present volume, part of which shows that Huxley's arrangement of the letters in his edition was sometimes wrong—a matter he could not always be held responsible for, since he had no access to the present collection. And in turn, some other letters from this period, coming to light in the future,

* *The Letters of D. H. Lawrence*, edited by Aldous Huxley (New York: The Viking Press, 1932). Itemized here as Huxley.

may show some of my own guesswork to be wrong. All that can be done now is to explain the basis of this guesswork.

I have put a date in brackets at the head of each undated letter. Naturally, the correspondence that Lawrence himself dated presented no problem. The first undated letter in this collection is the one designated Number 4. It has only 'Monday' on its dateline, but it was written at Greatham; since the Lawrences left Greatham in August 1915, it was obviously written before then. It presents few tangible clues; one of them is the notation, 'Thank you very much for the umbrella.' Since an umbrella is hardly the sort of thing one man would mail to another as a present, I assume that there must have been rain when Lawrence was leaving Russell's house in Cambridge at the end of his visit there, and that Russell must have given him an umbrella to use on the way to the station, telling him not to bother about returning it.

Since Letter Number 3, dated March 2, 1915, reveals that Lawrence was planning to visit Cambridge early in March, the umbrella reference helps to esablish Letter 4 as having been written during that month.

That Lawrence did not mention the Cambridge visit in Number 4 is no proof that this is not the first communication between the two men after that visit. Although Lawrence was not above writing a 'Collins,' as the Huxley collection shows, he did not always observe this custom. And that the Cambridge trip was a disappointment to him may be seen from the letter I have numbered 5, and from the one he wrote to Lady Ottoline Morrell, which appears on page 238 of the Huxley edition, as well as from Frieda Lawrence's report quoted in the Introduction to the present volume.

This Letter Number 4 was written on a Monday—by my guess, a week after Lawrence's return from Cambridge, on March 15. Russell perhaps wrote an answer to it, something to the effect that the university town and the people he met there must have depressed Lawrence, for in his 'Friday' letter—which I assume is Friday of that same week (March 19), and consequently Letter Number 5—Lawrence begins 'It is true Cambridge made me very black and down. I cannot bear its smell of rottenness, marsh-stagnancy . . .' and so on. Lawrence was usually outspoken and not hypocritical in these matters; that is why I take it for granted that instead of the usual 'Collins' he wrote Letter Number 4, saying merely he was sad and had not done much writing of his 'philosophy.' But now that Russell has brought up the subject of Cambridge, Lawrence in his Friday note ungraciously tells his recent host what he thinks of that host's environment. Also—for a bit more evidence—Lawrence still cannot go on with his 'philosophy'; he is still depressed. This is another link between those two letters I believe to have been written in the same week.

Letter Number 6 seems to have been written on Thursday, April 29. It is dated only 'Thrsday,' but mentions that Lawrence is going to London on (Saturday) May 8; later it says that

Lawrence hopes to see Russell there 'next weekend but one.' The 'next weekend but one' being that of May 8, the letter should have been written on Thursday, April 29.

The next letter requiring use of conjecture is that placed as Number 10. Since this one asks whether Russell is 'doing the lectures,' it must have been written before Lawrence's July 15 discussion of 'your lecture on the State,' and even before Lawrence's July 9 statement to Lady Ottoline, 'He sent me a synopsis of a set of lectures on Political Ideas.' (Huxley, p. 244.) And this Letter Number 10 seems to be later than Number 9, which Lawrence dated the 8th of June; in Number 9 and in the letters preceding, it is apparent that the idea of the lectures had not yet been born. Lawrence on June 8 was urging Russell to save himself for a bigger effort than that represented by his journalistic attacks on Lord Northcliffe. The two men must go deeper than Northcliffe, and beyond him: 'Let us wait a little while, till we can assemble the nucleus of a new belief, get a new centre of attack . . . [Y]ou are coming to us on the 19*th*. Then we will thresh out this business.'

Letter Number 8, June 2, also mentions the expected visit on the 19th. An undated letter in Huxley, to Lady Ottoline (page 242), placed amid the June and July correspondence, says 'Bertie Russell will come next Thursday, to stay till Saturday,' and the following letter, also to Lady Ottoline, says 'Bertie Russell is here.' This is dated 'Sunday'—Russell must either have arrived a day or so later than expected, or have stayed over.

June 20 was a Sunday that year; it is difficult not to believe that this letter to Lady Ottoline was not written on that day. After telling a bit about Russell, Lawrence goes on to say, 'We think to have a lecture hall in London in the autumn, and give lectures . . .' This evidence indicates that the notion of the lectures was first hit upon during the weekend of June 19-20, 1915.

This would certainly place Letter 10 *after* that date, and decidedly between Letter 9 (June 8) and Letter 11 (July 15). It is possible to investigate this Letter Number 10 further, and find good reasons for placing it in July. First, there is some internal evidence. Number 11, July 15, has strong resemblances, in its capital-and-labor passages, to the undated letter to Lady Ottoline on page 239 in Huxley. In this letter Lawrence said, 'The war is resolving itself into a war between Labour and Capital. Unless real leaders step forward, to lead in the light of a wide-embracing philosophy, there will be another French Revolution muddle.' Lawrence writes to Russell in the July 15 letter, 'This war is going to develop into the last great war between labour and capital. It will be a ghastly chaos of destruction, if it is left to Labour to be constructive. The fight must be given a higher aim than the triumph of Labour, or we shall have another French Revolution.'

The similarities of thought and expression here suggest that the two letters were written either on the same day or within a few days of each other, thereby making Huxley's placement of the one to Lady Ottoline—before June 1—erroneous (Huxley

of course lacked the evidence of the July 15 note to Russell).
It might be objected that the similarities quoted above merely
represented Lawrence's way of thinking during that entire summer, but the seasoned student of Lawrence's correspondence will
attest that Lawrence habitually used somewhat similar phrasing
in letters written on the same day or on successive days. And
during that summer of 1915, Lawrence was extremely protean
in his thought-processes, as an examination of the letters in the
present volume will indicate; he would hardly be using the same
expressions over any considerable period. In the foregoing quotations, the lines to Russell show at least a slight development
over those to Lady Ottoline: which does not mean that they
could not have been written immediately afterward.

On this evidence, I would date the quoted letter to Lady
Ottoline in July, and as close to the 15th (prior to it) as possible.
This dating is important in considering the present sequence of
Lawrence correspondence, for that same letter to Lady Ottoline
has further resemblances to another of the letters to Russell. In
this same specimen from page 239 of the Huxley collection, we
find Lawrence telling Lady Ottoline, 'I shall write all my philosophy again. Last time I came out of the Christian camp. This
time I must come out of these early Greek philosophers.' In
Letter Number 10 to Russell (which I am trying to establish as
belonging to the early part of July 1915), Lawrence says, 'I
have dropped writing my philosophy, but I go on working very
hard in my soul. I shall lift up my voice in the autumn, & in

connection with you, not apart. I have been wrong, much too Christian in my philosophy. These early Greeks have clarified my soul.'

The first statement in the last passage does not contradict what Lawrence had told Lady Ottoline, that he would write his philosophy again: the explanation to Russell is merely another version of that. And the duplicate statements about the influences of Christianity and the early Greeks suggest that once again there is a time-parity between two of these letters under consideration. Let it be said again that Lawrence was developing in a volatile fashion that summer and would hardly have held the same concepts of this kind over a long period of time, and that in any event a study of his letters will reveal that he was ordinarily not repetitious except in passages written on the same or on succeeding days.

Consequently I believe that the letter to Lady Ottoline on page 239 in Huxley, and Letters 10 and 11 in the Russell set, were all written within a few days of each other, with Number 11—dated July 15 and the only one with a date—as the latest of the three. Therefore I have dated Number 10 as having been written in July also. Lawrence put 'Wednesday' at the top of the letter; I have assumed that this is July 6, three days before Lawrence wrote Lady Ottoline Morrell that Russell had sent the synopsis of his lectures.

Letter 11 is merely dated '15 July,' and Lawrence did not give the year, but that is easily determined by the Greatham address, where the Lawrences resided from January to August of 1915.

Three more undated letters remain. The first of them is Number 17. Its superscription is 'Dec. 1915' and 'Monday.' The brevity of this letter makes its dating particularly difficult, but it can be accomplished. Its heading of 'Byron Villas, Hampstead,' places it before December 21 (on Monday, December 20, Lawrence had told Katherine Mansfield that he and his wife were leaving Hampstead on the following day). I would place the letter early in the month. On December 12, Lawrence was telling Katherine Mansfield that he and his wife planned to spend Christmas with his sister, a statement at odds with the one to Russell that he and his wife hoped to leave for America 'on the 24th of this month, if possible.' Lawrence also wrote Lady Ottoline Morrell on the 12th that he was leaving London on the 20th for his sister's place in Derbyshire. This statement also does not agree with the one in Letter 17 to Russell to the effect that Lawrence hoped to leave England by the 24th. He had told Murry on the 4th (Huxley, p. 292) that he hoped to leave England on the *Crown de Leone* on the 20th, and he had mentioned that ship and that date a day or so earlier in the letters to Lady Ottoline Morrell and Lady Cynthia Asquith dated (perhaps erroneously, as we shall see) on December 3. By Monday, December 6, that particular trip must have been called off, and the chance of another must have come into view: hence the mention of the 24th to Russell as a possible escape day. But by the 12th Lawrence was talking of Christmas in Derbyshire. I therefore place the Russell 'Monday' letter, Number 17, at December 6, 1915.

The next letter to be dated, Number 19, is headed: 'Ripley— Derby,' with 'Wednesday' as the only other given clue. The Derbyshire address should make this letter easy to date, since the Lawrences were up there only about a week—but, judging from the other letters of this period in the Huxley volume, dated by Lawrence himself, I can conclude only that Lawrence's personal calender was awry.

The wrongness begins in the first December letter in the Huxley volume, page 287, to Lady Cynthia, which Lawrence heads from Hampstead, 'Sunday, 3rd December, 1915.' The 3rd of December was a Friday in 1915.

In the comparative quiet of the Vale of Health, perhaps one day was like another: but Lawrence was not an absent-minded type—rather, he was alert and practical. How his calendar became so mixed, and stayed that way, is a mystery too deep for fathoming at this remove.

Another December 3 letter, on the page before, does not say 'Sunday,' and speaks of the visit that morning of Prince Bibesco. This is proof that the Lawrences had some contact with the outside world: it may be supposed that Prince Bibesco may have mentioned the day of the week, since there is a difference between a Sunday-morning call and a Friday-morning call. But Huxley may have put these two December 3 letters in the wrong order (indeed, several pages later he has a letter to Middleton Murry

[107]

and Katherine Mansfield, dated November 25, wrongly placed)—the one mentioning Prince Bibesco to Lady Ottoline Morrell may have been written in the afternoon, subsequent to Prince Bibesco's visit; the other one could have been written in the morning, before Prince Bibesco's arrival—since this letter was addressed to Lady Cynthia Asquith, it seems likely that Lawrence would have mentioned the prince. There is of course the possibility that the letters were written on two different days, one on (Friday) the 3rd, the other on Sunday (the 5th).

I have gone into this at some length in order to demonstrate how difficult it is to attempt to date the December 1915 letters. For Lawrence was inaccurate once again that month, when he dated a letter from Ripley to Lady Cynthia Asquith, 'Thursday, 24th December, 1915.' December 24 was a Friday. This is of especial concern here, since Letter Number 19 of the Russell series was possibly written during that week or the next. Another note of that week is puzzling as to exact date: the one to Lady Ottoline Morrell on page 301 in Huxley. This is headed 'Wednesday' only; it was postmarked '23 Dec., 15.' The 23rd was a Thursday—this letter, from '2 Hurst Close, Garden Suburb, N.W.,' may have been written on Wednesday the 22nd and may not have reached the post office till the following day.

It is hard, on the basis of the evidence within reach, to establish the date of the Lawrences' arrival in Derbyshire. It was possibly on the 22nd of December, more likely—in view of the postmark of the 23rd on the note to Lady Ottoline—on the

23rd or the 24th. The wrongly dated letter to Lady Cynthia ('Thursday, 24th December, 1915') may have been written on Thursday the 23rd, and the confusion in dates may be due to Lawrence's traveling on that day. In this case, however, I am more inclined to think that the letter to Lady Cynthia was written on *Friday* the 24th—a man coming to a house where there were small children, and a family gathering, should have known the *date* of the day before Christmas.

Lawrence had written Katherine Mansfield on the 20th that he would stay at his sister's till the 29th; and later we find him, in a correctly dated letter from Cornwall to Lady Cynthia ('Thursday, 30th December'—Huxley, p. 305), saying 'We came here tonight.' And in the preceding letter to Lady Ottoline Morrell (also correctly dated: 'Monday, 27 Dec., 1915'), Lawrence writes that he will go to Cornwall on Thursday. And in Letter Number 19 to Russell, he says 'We go to Cornwall on Thursday—30th.' He does not say 'tomorrow,' as he would if the 'Wednesday' referred to December 29. The only other Wednesday on which Lawrence could have been at Ripley was the 22nd; he could have written to Russell immediately after arriving. The colliers he mentions could have been seen by him on the way from the station. But the possibility that Lawrence had the day of the week wrong is so great that I am putting the date December 22-23, 1915 between brackets at the top of this letter.

The last item to be dealt with is Number 22. Lawrence gave

this letter no heading except 'Saturday.' Its salutation is 'My dear Russell,' like the Cornwall letters of February 11 and March 9. I believe it should be placed between these two.

Its references to Heseltine's fear of conscription and to his publishing scheme make it coeval with the February letters in the Huxley volume. And in Letter 21 to Russell, February 11, 1916, Lawrence had first spoken of the publishing scheme (a February 11 letter to Murry also mentions Heseltine's publishing ambitions to Murry for the first time; Huxley, p. 324) as it was working out, though he did not speak of Heseltine. But in Letter 22 he says, 'Heseltine is starting the publishing scheme' —which makes it naturally sequent to Letter 21.

But on which Saturday in February was this written? In the February 11 letter there is no mention of the Lawrences' moving; other references in the Huxley collection indicate that the Lawrences expected to use the Beresford place for another month. But apparently Beresford had written asking to have it back earlier, and the Lawrences seem to have left on February 29. In Letter 22 to Russell, Lawrence says, 'We have got to clear out of this place in a week's time. We are looking for another house.' I do not think this dates Letter 22 on Saturday, February 26, but rather on Saturday, February 19.

For on the 24th Lawrence wrote Beresford that they would leave on the following Tuesday; since this was the 29th, it was only five days away, and would have been only three days from the 26th. A letter (in Huxley) to Middleton Murry and Katherine Mansfield on February 17 shows that Lawrences apparently not expecting the Beresfords back until March 9—but between the 17th and the 19th, Beresford must have written Lawrence that he would like to have the cottage back by the first of March. So Lawrence tells Russell that he and Mrs. Lawrence have to move out in a week. Also, if Letter 22 had been written on Saturday the 26th, it would have come after the one to Beresford on the 24th, and in that letter Lawrence states that he has found a house near Zennor, St. Ives. But in Letter 22 he is looking for a house.

Further corroboration is given by Lawrence's letter to Lady Ottoline on February 15, 1916 (Huxley, p. 326 ff.), saying that a letter had just come in from 'Bertie,' who was miserable, lived only for trivialities, etc. 'I feel sorry for him, but my heart doesn't soften to him just yet. . . .' Surely *this* letter from Russell is the one Lawrence is answering in the first paragraph of Number 22; and the ship metaphor seems a continuation of the one he had used, more grimly, in the February 7 letter to Lady Ottoline. (Huxley, p. 321.) Therefore the 'Saturday' in the Lawrence letter which I have numbered 22 must be Saturday, February 19, 1916.

Lawrence would have mocked at all this doctor-of-philosophizing about the dates of his letters, but for the sake of those who want to read this correspondence in its correct sequence, the elaborate explanations are necessary.

[111]